Landscapes of the
SOUTH OF
FRANCE
2 ■ Aix to the Pyrenees

a countryside guide

John and Pat Underwood

D1332348

SUNFLOWER
BOOKS

First published 1995
by Sunflower Books
12 Kendrick Mews
London SW7 3HG, UK

ISBN 1-85691-058-X

The Roman theatre, Arles

Important note to the reader

We have tried to ensure that the descriptions and maps in this book are error-free at press date. The book will be updated, where necessary, whenever future printings permit. It will be very helpful for us to receive your comments (sent in care of the publishers, please) for the updating of future printings. We also rely on those who use this book — especially walkers — to take along a good supply of common sense when they explore. Conditions can change fairly rapidly, and **storm damage or bulldozing may make a route unsafe at any time**. If the route is not as we outline it here, and your way ahead is not secure, return to the point of departure. **Never attempt to complete a tour or walk under hazardous conditions!** Please read carefully the Country code on page 11, the notes on pages 71 to 74, and the introductory comments at the beginning of each tour and walk (regarding road conditions, equipment, grade, distances and time, etc). Explore **safely**, while at the same time respecting the beauty of the countryside.

Cover: Roussillon
Title page: Village signpost in Hérault
Photographs by John Underwood
Touring maps by John Theasby and Pat Underwood
Walking maps adapted from IGN Série Bleue 1:25,000 maps with the permission of the Institut Géographique National
A CIP catalogue record for this book is available from the British Library.
Printed and bound in the UK by KPC Group, Ashford, Kent

10 9 8 7 6 5 4 3 2 1

Contents

Walking   71
Weather; What to take; Nuisances;
Waymarking, grading, safety; Maps

Young cherry trees planted out south of Murs, with the Lubéron rising through haze in the background. A example of the perfect harmony between man and nature that is the secret of the French countryside.

 Preface

This two-volume *Landscapes of the South of France* will plunge you into the most beautiful countryside between the Alps and the Pyrenees. Nature has prepared the canvas for these landscapes over millions of years, but man has added colour, form and texture. The straight bold strokes of lavender, vineyards, planes and poplars streak across plateaux; bridges and aqueducts arc gracefully over rivers; sturdy stone towers with whimsical wrought-iron bell-cages stipple the hilltops.

If the harmony between man and nature is the key to the beauty of this countryside, nowhere is it better conveyed than in the paintings of the Impressionists and Post-Impressionists so intimately associated with the South of France — Cézanne, Van Gogh, Monet. Almost everywhere you travel a masterpiece comes to life — an isolated farmhouse awash in fields of scarlet poppies, the limestone ribs of Ste-Victoire rising above a bib of emerald vineyards, stars burning out in a cobalt blue sky over the lamplit lanes of Arles.

This is a guide to the outdoors, written for those who prize the countryside as highly as a cathedral. We want to take you along the most beautiful roads by car and, when the opportunity presents itself, park, don walking boots, pick up the rucksack and *participate* in this landscape. France caters marvellously for all grades of walkers, but *precise* descriptions of tours and walks for motorists are rare. Most touring guides concentrate on

Unlike the Pont du Gard, this gem of a Roman aqueduct near Ansignan is still being used to irrigate vineyards. It makes a wonderful picnic setting along the route of Car tour 11, 'Towards the Pyrenees'.

history and architecture, while books for walkers outline the famous long-distance routes (the Grandes Randonnées). But these 'GR' footpaths are sometimes very demanding and, being linear, are in any case unsuitable for motorists.

Our aim has been to describe the **tours** so precisely that you will not need to make *constant* reference to a map. The **walks** chosen — from the vast network of possible routes — are those we feel offer the greatest sense of satisfaction for the effort involved.

The first volume of *Landscapes of the South of France* travels from the Alps to Aix-en-Provence. This book will take you through western Provence and Languedoc-Roussillon to Canigou, sacred mountain of the Pyrenees. From there *Landscapes of the Pyrenees* could accompany you all the way to the Atlantic coast.

Bibliography

It must be stressed that this is a *countryside* guide, meant to be used in conjunction with a standard guide or guides covering the area. The Michelin guides are indispensable, and to accompany this book you would need the following:

Michelin Red Guide: *always travel with the **latest** edition.* Not only is it useful for finding accommodation (and telephoning ahead), but the town plans are *essential* for finding your way round the cities. *Note that all our car tours refer to Michelin town exit numbers.*

Michelin Green Guides: Provence (available in English), **Gorges du Tarn** (in French only); **Pyrénées Roussillon** (optional; only available in French).

Of the plethora of guides on the market, the **Cadogan Guide to the South of France** matches most closely the territory covered in the two volumes of *Landscapes of the South of France;* its presentation and suggestions for places to stay should appeal to 'Landscapers'.

You will need a good flora; a paperback is handiest when walking, but we must confess to lugging the massive **Mediterranean Wild Flowers** (Blamey and Grey-Wilson, Harper Collins).

At the top of each **car tour** we refer to the appropriate **Michelin maps** (yellow series; scale 1:200,000). For this book you will need maps 80, 81, 83, 84 and 86 *or* the larger-format maps 240 (Languedoc/ Roussillon), 235 (Midi-Pyrénées) and 245 (Provence/Côte d'Azur); you may like to supplement these with the larger-scale map 114 (French Riviera/Var; scale 1:100,000).

For **walking** we hope that you will find the IGN maps reproduced here sufficient. If you wish to explore an area in more detail, IGN maps are widely available. Beside each map we give the appropriate number, if you want to do more walking in the area. We cannot recommend too strongly that you take advantage of the wealth of *free material* available from the local tourist offices. You should be able to get up-to-date sketch maps of local walks almost anywhere you go. But before using this material, make sure that you can form a mental picture of the walk in advance — the climb, the distance, the terrain. Read carefully what we say about this material on page 73, under 'Waymarking, grading, safety'.

From the Chapelle St-Christophe you look out west over vineyards to Mont Ventoux. This pine-scented perch makes a delightful picnic spot during Car tour 3, but it's only one of the truly fabulous settings en route in Walk 5, a spectacular hike which takes you into the heart of the Dentelles de Montmirail and the Gigondas vineyards.

Picnicking

Picnicking possibilities are limitless in the South of France — especially if you follow the example of the locals and tour with a collapsible table and chairs (available at very low cost in the supermarkets). Picnic areas with tables are encountered on some of the tours; these are indicated in the touring notes and on the touring map with the symbol ⊼. All the walks in the book offer superb picnic settings but, on days when you are planning *only* to tour by car, it is helpful to have some idea of the best places for a lunch break en route. All of the selections below are *arranged by car tour*, and very few involve any walking, so you won't be delayed from 'sightseeing'. All these picnic spots, favourites of ours over the years, are highlighted on the touring map, with a *P* printed in white. Where possible we have chosen places where there is something firm and dry to sit on.

CAR TOUR 1: The Lure mountain is climbed about halfway through the tour. At the chapel of **Notre-Dame-de-Lure** (⊼; photograph page 10) you will find shaded tables and benches, or you can sit on the chapel steps. At the end of the tour follow Short walk 1 (page 75), to picnic in **Roussillon's ocre quarries** (photograph page 76); there is ample shade and plenty of room to get away from other visitors.

CAR TOUR 2: There are delightful settings on the Lubéron, but nothing to sit on. The **Combe de Vidauque** (early in the tour) offers superb views from a rock garden of wild flowers, but no shade. As you climb to the **Forêt des Cèdres** (over halfway through the tour) you could park 3km uphill: superb views over Lacoste and Bonnieux; some shade. There are no views at the cedar forest on the summit, but it is cool and sweet-scented. Also **Roussillon** at the end of the tour (see Car tour 1).

St-Sixte (Car tour 5). From the rocks behind this 12th-century chapel, there is a fine view to Eygalières and the Alpilles. Chapels are almost invariably good picnic spots because there is usually somewhere to sit and shade nearby. Rivers also make attractive picnic settings (sometimes with an ancient bridge adjacent), so we often aim for a river crossing. The only disadvantage is the seasonal onslaught of mosquitoes and gnats. Unfortunately, this is also true around lakes.

8

CAR TOUR 3: As you descend the **northern flanks of Ventoux** there are lovely shaded places to pull off the road, but nothing to sit on (it is also *very cold* here, so picnicking would only be enjoyable in very hot weather). At the bottom of the descent you pass the chapel of **Notre-Dame-du-Groseau**, the beautifully-kept chancel of an 11c Benedictine abbey, with stone seating round a shaded grassy 'courtyard'. This holy place reputedly dates back to pre-Celtic times, when a nearby spring was revered; *please preserve the silence and leave nothing behind.* The **Col du Cayron** in the Dentelles de Montmirail offers stones to sit on and shade. From the col you can turn right on a motorable track (behind a sign warning that you proceed at your own risk) to the Rocher du Midi viewpoint (⊟); or turn left and park below the St-Christophe chapel (see map on pages 86-87; photographs pages 7, 28, 85). Also **Roussillon** at the end of the tour (see Car tour 1).

CAR TOUR 4: The **Pont Julien**, a Roman bridge, is crossed halfway through the tour. You can sit on rocks beside the Calavon; there is shade nearby. At the end of the tour the banks of the Gard on either side of the **Pont du Gard** make idyllic picnic spots. On the *south* side of the bridge you will find rocks to sit on. And what better view could you have than the one shown on pages 46-47?

CAR TOUR 5: Halfway through the tour there are several picnic places, all with pleasant, if not spectacular, views. If you drive just 200m past the **Le Destet** turn-off, there is a shaded picnic spot on the left beside a wide irrigation canal. Perch on the side of the canal if you have no chairs. The **D24 from Le Destet to Eygalières** offers excellent pine-shaded picnic spots by the roadside. You can sit on the wall at the **St-Sixte** chapel (photograph below; limited shade). A very popular spot with the local people is the pine-shaded lake just south of **St-Rémy**, where Walk 8 begins (see 'How to get there' on page 92). Also the **Pont du Gard** at the end of the tour (see Car tour 4).

CAR TOUR 6: Shade is hard to come by in the Camargue, and (in our experience) most areas are plagued by biting insects. If you have a beach umbrella, the daisy-encrusted dunes at the **Plage de Piémanson** make an idyllic beach setting, unless the day is very windy.

CAR TOUR 7: The tables and benches beside the bubbling Hérault at **Laroque** (halfway through the tour; ⚲) make an attractive setting. If you have time and don't mind a short walk, the ruined hamlet of **Montcalmès** is a gorgeous shady spot. This involves a 4km return detour from Puéchabon, near the end of the tour, and a walk of 35 minutes each way: follow Short walk 10, page 99.

CAR TOUR 8: As you head north along the **river Hérault**, you can picnic on rocks by the Pont du Diable (30km; photograph page 71) or below another bridge some 25km further north (opposite the chapel of St-Etienne-d'Issensac). The municipal park at **Brissac** (photograph page 49) has shaded benches. The banks of the **river Vis** at Navacelles offer shade. If you don't mind a walk, leave your car by the river bank and walk back uphill to the fork where the D130 goes to ST-MAURICE, then follow Walk 11 for 20 minutes. Near the end of the tour, the grassy slopes near the *lavogne* (paved watering hole) at **La Couvertoirade** are pleasant, but offer little shade.

CAR TOUR 9: At the start of the tour there are four excellent picnic places. Just short of Octon, you can turn off left to the **Lac du Salagou** (shaded ⚲; overview photograph pages 108-109). At La Lieude you can climb to the **Château de Malavieille** (photograph page 107; allow 30min); rocks to sit on; shade from the castle walls. **La Mouline** (photograph page 57), a little further on, is an idyllic setting with ample parking, but there is no shade, nor anywhere to perch. In contrast, at the **Cirque de Mourèze** (photograph opposite) you will find plenty of shade and rocks to sit on. About halfway through the tour, the **Gorges d'Héric** (photograph page 112) make a fantastic setting; *allow plenty of time* and see Short walks, page 111.

CAR TOUR 10: Just under halfway through the tour the **Roc Suzadou** is a fine viewpoint over the Cesse Valley (⚲; little shade). At the end of the tour, there are ⚲ at Trèbes beside the **Canal du Midi**, or follow Short walk 18 to picnic in the setting shown on page 125.

CAR TOUR 11: There are two very pleasant picnic spots halfway through the tour. At the **Grau de Maury**, opposite the road to Quéribus, there is a short track to a stone shelter. The two trees here

Notre-Dame-de-Lure. Ancient trees shade this small chapel, built above the remains of a simple 12th-century monastery. According to legend, there was a hermitage near this site as early as the 5th century.

The aptly-named Sphinx in the Cirque de Mourèze

provide *the only shade* for miles around, and there is a fine view over to Quéribus. You can get to the **banks of the Verdouble** by turning right just before Duilhac (see large-scale map page 129). After 1.6km park and picnic by a ruined bridge. (Or wade across the river and walk up the 'marble riverbed' shown on page 128, to the waterfalls). If you follow the tour towards the Pyrenees, you will pass two superb sites. The first is the setting shown on page 68, a ruined farm on the D619 north of Catlar, near the **Pic de Baou** (ample shade; rocks to sit on). Some 10km further on the tour visits the **Roman aqueduct at Ansignan** shown on page 6. Sit on the aqueduct or under it; the arches provide the only shade.

A country code for walkers and motorists

Bear in mind that all land in the South of France is privately owned, whether by an individual or a district. All waymarked walks and other routes described in this book are permissive, *not* 'rights of way'. Behave responsibly, never forgetting the danger of forest fires.

- **Do not light fires** except at purpose-built barbecues. *Never park your car blocking a fire-fighting track!*
- **Do not frighten animals**. When driving, always stop the car until the livestock have moved off the road.
- **Walk quietly** through all farms, hamlets and villages, **leaving any gates just as you find them.**
- **Protect all wild and cultivated plants.** Don't pick wild flowers or uproot saplings. Obviously crops are someone's livelihood and should not be touched. **Never walk over cultivated land!**
- **Take all your litter away with you.**
- **Stay on the path.** Don't take short cuts on zigzag paths; this damages vegetation and hastens erosion, eventually destroying the main path.

✻ Touring

The 11 car tours in this second volume of *Landscapes of the South of France* take you west from Aix through Languedoc-Roussillon to the eastern Pyrenees. While a few important centres have been omitted for lack of space, we feel that the two books present a comprehensive overview of the most beautiful landscapes.

The touring notes are brief: they include little history or information readily available in other publications (see Bibliography, page 6). *We concentrate instead on route planning:* each tour has been devised to follow **the most beautiful roads** in the relevant region and to take you to the starting point of some delightful **walks**. (Further information about some of the places visited can be found in the notes for the walks.)

The large fold-out map is designed to give you a quick overview of the touring routes, walks and picnic places *in both volumes.* At the start of each tour we refer to the relevant Michelin touring map(s), but we hope that our very detailed notes will enable you to tour *without constant reference to a map* — avoiding eyestrain and friction between driver and navigator.

Signposting *to be followed* is always shown in SMALL CAPITALS. We give explicit directions for getting through villages, but *not* cities (where new roundabouts and signposting are frequently encountered). ***Important:*** *Both driver and navigator should look over the* **latest** *Michelin Red Guide* **before** *entering or leaving any large city,* so that you have some idea of where you are heading and landmarks en route. It is *never* as simple as it looks on the touring maps, and *hours* can be wasted twirling in spaghetti hoops on ring roads round cities like Aix or Nîmes!

Early morning at Navacelles (Car tour 8)

12

Because this is a *countryside* guide, the tours often bypass the villages en route, however beautiful or historically important. We do, however, use symbols to alert you to the cultural highlights (a **key to the symbols** used is on the touring map, but note also the following abbreviations: R Romanesque; G Gothic; C classical).

Some other points to keep in mind: **petrol stations** are often closed on Sundays and holidays in the remote areas covered by some of the tours. **Cyclists** do *not* travel in single file, nor is cycling confined to weekends. But on Sundays some roads will be closed off for cycle races: you will have to take a short *déviation*. *Déviations*, however, are *not* short when they involve roadworks. Especially in spring, long stretches of road will be closed, and you may have to go up to 50km out of your way! French **arrow signposting** is mystifying until you get used to it (another reason why we give very detailed instructions). Finally, remember that **Sundays and holidays** are a nightmare at the most popular 'sights'; monuments like the Pont du Gard or Les Baux should be avoided at all costs. Our tours have been planned not only to take you via the most beautiful roads, but to reach the three-star attractions before or after the crowds. If you follow our advice, but you *still* encounter crowds, we must confess: we would never visit the South of France in July or August ...

Tour 1: NATURE TAMED BY INDUSTRY

**Aix-en-Provence • Rochers des Mées • Sisteron •
St-Etienne-les-Orgues • Montagne de Lure • Banon •
Simiane-la-Rotonde • (Rustrel) • Apt • Roussillon**

*255km/158mi; about 7h driving; Michelin map 84 (or larger-scale
map 114) to begin, then map 81*

En route: ⊞ on the A51 motorway, Rochers des Mées; *P* at Notre-
Dame-de-Lure (⊞), Roussillon's ocre quarries; Walk 1; also Walks 17
and 18 in the companion volume *(South of France: The Alps to Aix)*

*Because this is a very long tour, we use the motorway to start. If you
abhor motorways, or if you can break the tour into two days, take the
N96 from Aix, make a detour to Forcalquier and the Observatoire de
Haute-Provence, then rejoin our tour at the Rochers des Mées.
Sisteron would be a good place to break the tour. The road to the
Signal de Lure is very narrow and winding and becomes vertiginous
above tree-line; on Sundays and in high season nervous drivers and
passengers may prefer to turn back after Notre-Dame-de-Lure.*

The Durance rises near Briançon, a frothing Alpine
stream. By the time it has raged through to the
Mediterranean basin, the now-wide river runs sluggishly
over its pebbly bed, tamed by the many dams and
canals which today control its flow, watering the thirsty
soil of Provence and powering many new industries.
From the weird metallic beauty of the modern industrial
landscape rising on the banks of this milky-turquoise
river, we move on to a totally different 'industrial'
landscape — the ocre quarries of Vaucluse.

Our journey west to the Pyrenees begins at **Aix-en-
Provence** (described, with walk suggestions, in *South of
France: The Alps to Aix*). Leave Aix by ①, the N96, and
after 6km join the A51 motorway north at junction 12.
Cross the Canal EDF (Electricité de France), one of the
most important canals fed by the Durance. A sign tells
us we have entered the Lubéron, and the mountain is
seen ahead, straddling the horizon. The motorway
curves round to head east, with the Durance on our left,
but the river isn't glimpsed until near Pont-Mirabeau
(⊞), where a picnic area overlooks the pebbly riverbed
and desultory streams of turquoise water. At 44km we
cross the Durance just west of its confluence with the
Verdon (its last major tributary); the small Barrage de
Cadarache is on the right. Under 3km further on we are
welcomed into the Alpes-de-Haute-Provence. On the
west side of the river wide fields, with enormous
gantries for watering, fill the space between the honey-
coloured village of Ste-Tulle and the spread of Valence.
Come to the Aire de Manosque (⊞⊞) and its strange
'sculptures', characteristic of French motorway picnic

14

The Rochers des Mées, or 'The Penitents'. According to legend, they are robed monks, turned to stone by St Donatus. Their crime was to lust after beautiful Moorish women kidnapped by early 'crusaders'.

areas. There is a fine view over the wide riverbed and frayed stream here; one can easily imagine how destructive the river could be before it was harnessed. The motorway crosses the wide Canal d'Oraison, which in turn crosses the Durance on our right.

At 70km leave the motorway at Exit 19: bear right for FORCALQUIER and ORAISON. Beyond the *péage* go right on the D4B for ORAISON. Cross the spectacular riverbed and turn left on the D4 for DABISSE and LES MEES. The attractive road passes through a flat agricultural plain. In **Dabisse** watch for a tiled dovecot on the left and a lovely grove of poplars. Bypass **Les Mées** (on the left; the church has a very attractive wrought-iron bell-cage). Follow TOUTES DIRECTIONS and then SISTERON on the D4, passing the **Rochers des Mées★** on the right (◉⋒). Some of these weirdly-eroded rocks (see above) rise to 150m/500ft. Unfortunately, there is no shade at the picnic area.

At 95km, having crossed the impressive Pont Canal and then the Bléone, we come to a roundabout and go straight over for DIGNE. At another roundabout, 1.5km further on, follow SISTERON by taking the second exit, the N85 (the 'Route Napoléon'; Car tour 4 in the *Alps to Aix* volume). Cross the fast-flowing Pont Canal again and then keep it on your right. On the left, in the distance, is the large lump of the Montagne de Lure. Just before the N85 crosses the Durance, turn right on the D4 for L'ESCALE and VOLONNE. Cross the Pont Canal for a third time and, just beyond it, fork left. Beyond **L'Escale** you climb above the Durance — note its

15

stronger flow as you head north. In **Volonne** bear left at a Y-fork for TOUTES DIRECTIONS; then, at the lights, keep straight ahead for SISTERON on the D4. Climb to a plateau cultivated with cereals and other crops, below a backdrop of mountains. The remains of the 11CR chapel of St-Martin stand off to the right on a hill.

Crest a rise and look ahead to Sisteron. Below is the dam where the canal takes its water. On coming to a roundabout, take the *first exit* for GAP and GRENOBLE. Once through the Tunnel de la Baume, pull up left at a viewpoint★ (📷) towards Sisteron, with its 12/16c citadel rising on a sheer buttress of rock (photograph below). Some 3km further on turn left for CENTRE VILLE and cross the Durance. Drive through a tunnel beneath the citadel and then bear right on a plane tree avenue. Park and stroll around **Sisteron★** (115km ✝🛏ⓘ), a good overnight base. Aside from the citadel, be sure to see the former cathedral (Notre-Dame-des-Pommiers, 12CR) and the clock tower with its lovely wrought-iron bell-cage. A key staging-post throughout history, Sisteron was on the Via Domitia linking the Alps with the Rhône Delta; almost 1500 years later, Napoléon stopped here for lunch on his triumphal return from exile on Elba.

The next part of the tour visits the Montagne de Lure, which *can* be approached from just outside Sisteron. We do not recommend this route, however: not only is the north side of the mountain less attractive, but the road is often in *very poor* condition, vertiginous, and prone to rock-falls. We head south from Sisteron, leaving from ②, the N85 for DIGNE and AIX. After about 5km bear right on the D951 for PEIPIN and ST-ETIENNE. After passing to the right of **Peipin**, notice the necklace of low grey hillocks on the left, set off by a collar of colourful fields. Small stands of trees further enhance this unusual landscape. Beyond the vivid green fields of attractive **Les Paulons** you come to **Châteauneuf** and bear right with the D951 for ST-ETIENNE. Pass the church on the left and then turn left for PEYRUIS on the D801, a country lane. Some 4.5km from Châteauneuf meet the D101 and go left, again for PEYRUIS. Soon the 14CR pilgrimage church of St-Donat★ (✝) is seen on a wooded hillside to the right. This well-restored example of early Romanesque art

The approach to Sisteron on the D4

rises on the site where the hermit saint (whose monks pay penance at Les Mées) retired in the 6th century.

Return to the last junction and fork left. Now the Lure mountain is a big green mound ahead. Pass a massive quarry, meet the D951 again, and turn left. Beyond **Mallefougasse** a wide valley opens up on the left. **Cruis** is a gorgeous honey-coloured hamlet with a simple church. The beautiful valley road, bordered by fields, takes us to **St-Etienne-les-Orgues** (150km 13/18c⬚ ℹ️🅿️), where some of the 16c houses lean out over the road. This is your last chance to get petrol for some 40km. Pass to the right of the church with its pointed spire and bear right on the D413 (D113 on Michelin maps) to climb the **Montagne de Lure★**. Crawl up in hairpin bends through lavender fields and then a forest of mixed conifers. About 10km uphill, not far beyond a shrine on the left, turn right along a potholed track to **Notre-Dame-de-Lure** (161km 12c⛪P🌲; photograph page 10). This site is also associated with St Donatus, who founded a hermitage near here in the 5th century.

Return to the D413 and turn right uphill, passing a refuge on the right and then a hotel and ski-run (which unhappily disfigure the landscape in summer). At the Y-fork go either way; the roads rejoin. Now, having climbed above tree-line, you can enjoy wonderful views down off the white scree-slopes of the mountain, dotted with dwarf junipers. From a pass you look out toward the snow-capped Alps. The road is noticeably vertiginous now; the edge is not built up at the side. Pass the road to the Signal de Lure (1826m/6000ft) and come over another pass — to fine, if hazy, views of Mont Ventoux, the Cévennes, the Alps and the coast. Turn round here, back to St-Etienne (193km).

Now head west again on the D951. Pass two tiny chapels on the right, St-Joseph and St-Sebastien. The valley of the Laye below on the left is a patchwork of

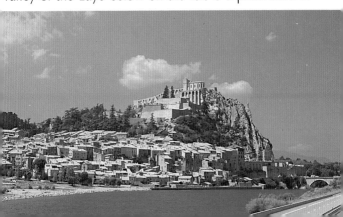

colour studded with stands of poplars and low stone farm buildings. Ignore the right turn to Ongles; go left for BANON. Not far beyond some mellow red and ochre buildings up on the right, turn right for BANON on the D950, through rolling hillocks and emerald cultivation. Set like a tiny gem on the right is honey-hued **Le Largue**, its tiny church weighed down by two large bells in a wall-belfry. Pass the R chapel of Notre-Dame-des-Anges on a hillock to the right and soon turn left with the D950 for BANON; then go right immediately. In the lower village of **Banon** ignore the D950 to Revest, go round the roundabout (a brick wall encircling a hedge) and take the next turn-off *(not signposted)*. Then, at a fork, bear right. The old part of the village, with its rainbow of shutters, is perched up on the right. Now, unless you want to stop for some of its renowned goats' cheese wrapped in chestnut leaves, turn left at the T-junction. This puts you on the D51 for SIMIANE.

You cross a plateau. Rows of lavender paint attractive stripes in the landscape at any time of year and lead the eye up right to gorgeous **Simiane-la-Rotonde★** (⬚). Honey-coloured houses spill down the hill from the focal point — the eponymous rotunda, all that remains of the 12c château/dungeon of the counts of Simiane.

Continue on the wooded D51; it becomes the D22 when you enter Vaucluse. Soon the Calavon Valley opens up on the left — a Swiss-Alpine landscape, with rolling green hills and a lake. At a fork turn right for APT and AVIGNON, following the Dôa. Soon the ochre quarries of the **Colorado Provençal★** are seen to the left, adding colour and texture to the tapestry of fields.*

Come into **Apt** (244km ⓘ), cross the Calavon, and turn right immediately for AVIGNON, CAVAILLON (Exit ③, the N100). After 4.5km turn right on the D4. Then go left on the D104 into crimson **Roussillon★** (255km ⓘ*P*), perched atop the gouged-out ochre quarries shown on page 76. One of the most beautiful villages in Provence, Roussillon (see cover photograph) is a fine touring base. And Walk 1 is an easy introduction to this extravaganza of colour, best seen under a low sun.

*Soon you could turn right for Rustrel and from there follow the D30 (Sault road) for a short distance, to overlook the Colorado (and the Lubéron) from a higher vantage point. *A word of warning:* You may have heard that there is good walking in the Colorado, but unless you have all day to spend getting lost in a maze of quarries, it is best avoided. There is *no signposting or waymarking,* and *many of the paths are dangerous.* Note also: admission is paid.

Tour 2: THE LUBERON

Roussillon • Forêt de Venasque • Abbaye de Sénanque • Gordes • Combe de Vidauque • Abbaye de Silvacane • Cadenet • Forêt des Cèdres • Saignon • Roussillon

166km/103mi; about 6h driving; Michelin maps 81 and 84, or 245

En route: 🄵 at Forêt de Venasque, Côtes de Sénanque; **P** at Combe de Vidauque, Forêt des Cèdres, Roussillon; Walks 1, 2, 3, 4

Roads are varied — some narrow and winding, others wide and fairly busy. In places the road from the Forêt de Venasque to the Abbaye de Sénanque is only wide enough for one car, and you may have to back up for touring coaches. This is a good reason to set out early.

The Lubéron, a 60km/37mi-long wooded massif, stretches east to west in the cradle of the Durance between Manosque and Avignon. Seen from a distance, the range betrays nothing of its limestone crags and ravines; it rises gently off the plain in one great mass of emerald greenery. Its shape is unmistakable — reminiscent of a giant cat in slumber. Whatever time of year you climb its flanks, nature will put on a superb display: the lavender fields of Sénanque and the Vaucluse Plateau are best seen in high summer, the Combe de Vidauque in late spring, and the foothills in autumn, when the vineyards weave a tapestry of reds and golds.

Leave **Roussillon** on the D227 (ST SATURNIN, MURS, APT). Join the D4 and turn left for MURS, CARPENTRAS. The road winds through orchards and vineyards (photograph pages 4-5) but, as you reach the Plateau de Vaucluse, *garrigues* take over. Soon **Murs** stretches out ahead (🄼); a delicate wrought-iron bell-cage and the 16c castle with bartizans are visible. Pass below the centre and keep ahead, ignoring the right turn for Sault. Your route (D4 to VENASQUE) is not signposted until you are leaving Murs. There is a superb view left towards the western or 'Petit' Lubéron, with orchards and farmlands in the foreground, just before the Col de Murs.

Continue downhill through the oaks of the **Forêt de Venasque**. Soon you're in a grey-rock gorge (🄵), which is dry for most of the year. At the next crossroads turn left on the D177 for GORDES, ABBAYE DE SENANQUE *(or first continue ahead to Venasque, to see one of the oldest religious buildings in France, the 6c Merovingian baptistery; a detour of 8km return)*. The D177 follows a more impressive gorge (best seen in autumn for the foliage), but it too is dry for most of the year. When the D244 comes in from the left, continue ahead for GORDES, winding down the Sénancole Valley through mixed woodlands. On the approach there is a superb view () over fields of lavender to the isolated 12CR **Abbaye de Sénanque★** (31.5km ✝). Walk 2 passes this way; see photograph page 78. Sénanque is one of three important Cistercian abbeys in Provence, a 'sister' to the Abbaye de Silvacane (visited later in the tour) and Le Thoronet (a detour on Car tour 8 in *South of France: The Alps to Aix*).

From the abbey the road to Gordes is very narrow but, if there are no cars or coaches around, you can pull up in a passing bay for more superb views down onto the abbey's setting. At 32km, at the Côtes de Sénanque (from where the GR6 descends to Gordes), there's an excellent view down over the plain towards the Petit Lubéron (📷 and ☂ 0.7km downhill). Now you enter the world of the 'bories' and the beautiful, incredibly intricate dry-stone walls that surround Gordes (see photograph and notes page 23, and Walk 2).

At 34km turn left to enter **Gordes★** (🏛M🛈), a lively

Plane tree avenues filtering out the intense heat of the sun create one of the most memorable landscapes in the South of France.

town with a good market. The plethora of craft shops attests to heavy tourist traffic. The Renaissance château (where Walk 2 starts) houses a Vasarely museum and the tourist office. But what you are most likely to remember about Gordes is its magnificent setting when seen from the south: it rises from the plateau like an acropolis. Watch for this view: it comes up *behind you* as you leave the village on the D15 for CAVAILLON. On meeting the D2 bear right, again following CAVAILLON. *To visit the Village des Bories (photograph page 23), go right again at the traffic lights 100m further on.*

In **Coustellet** (lavender **M**), cross straight over the N100. The Petit Lubéron rises straight ahead. Pass the D144 left to Ménerbes and enter **Robion**. Go through two sets of traffic lights and, just after the *second* set of lights, turn left for LES TAILLADES. Soon the Canal de Carpentras is on the left. Beyond a mill with a working water wheel, where the D143 goes right to Cavaillon, follow CHEVAL-BLANC, staying on the D31. Attractive cane wind-breaks line both sides of the road, and the canal soon reappears on the left. Ignore the left turn to Vidauque, and *now watch for your turn-off, which is not currently signposted.* Just 0.6km past the Vidauque road, turn sharp left: a tall hedge of firs will be on your left and pines on your right. At a fork, go sharp right uphill. There is a sign here, ROUTE DES CRETES; MONTEE DE VIDAUQUE. The road ahead is one-way for the next 3km.

Now climb the **Combe de Vidauque★** past various laybys (📷), including a fine viewpoint over Cavaillon at the foot of Mont St-Jacques (if you've ever tried to drive through Cavaillon, the largest vegetable market in France, you may agree with us that this is the best way to see the town). The beautiful agricultural valley of the Durance glimmers below a backdrop of distant mountains. *Note:* the most impressive views of the Lubéron rising before you and the plain below are on the *lower* part of this road, so pull up where you can before you climb too high. Almost before you notice it, the slumbering Lubéron springs to life: shaking off its green mantle, the mountain reveals rippling ribs of grey limestone. If you come in spring, reach for the flora: you may be able to find half the entries in it on this short stretch of road. You have climbed into an unbelievably beautiful rock garden, a rainbow of wild flowers (**P**).

The Tête des Buisses (619m) on the left marks the top of the climb at 58km, and your descent begins ... down the 'Rat's Hole' (le Trou-du-Rat). ***Beware:*** *Although it is shown as a one-way road on the Michelin map,* **from here on this narrow road is two-way***.* Sweet-scented pines perfume the dramatic descent to the Durance Valley, where bamboos, conifers and poplars shield a cornucopia of cultivation beside the turquoise river. Just before the main road, pass a shaded picnic area with a lovely brook, but no tables. Cross the Canal de Carpentras and go left on the D973. *(Turn now to map 84.)*

The heights of the Lubéron become more impressive again, as we head east, skirting the canal. Some 2km past the pretty entrance to the Gorges du Régalon on the left, turn right on the D32 for MALLEMORT. Go under shady acacias and cross the Durance (look right here, to see an interesting old suspension bridge). Enter Bouches-du-Rhône, where the road is numbered D23E. At the roundabout go straight over for SENAS. Join the N7 and turn left for AIX *(dangerous junction)*. Plane trees line one side of the road, cane the other. Cross the wide Canal EDF and, 1.5km further on, turn left on the D561. Beyond **Charleval** (ⓘ) cross the Canal de Marseille (wide turquoise canals are a prominent feature of this tour, as they were on Tour 1) and bear right for ABBAYE DE SILVACANE. In **La Roque** go straight ahead, just to the left of the church. On coming to a fork, keep left on the main road for the 12CR **Abbaye de Silvacane★** (92km ♣), with shady parking on the right. As at Sénanque, the simplicity of the buildings is most impressive. St Bernard, who inspired the Cistercians, believed that saintliness could only come about through a life simply led, in poverty and isolation. All monastic buildings were to be pure in line and lacking in ornamentation. Think back to the isolated site of Sénanque; at its founding, Silvacane was equally isolated: this area was desolate, save for a 'forest of reeds' (*Sylva cana*).

Leaving the abbey, continue in the same direction. After 1.5km, when you meet the main D561, go right for APT. Just under 2km further on turn left on the D943 for CADENET. Cross the Canal EDF and then the Durance, which is just a mass of pebbles here, and come into Vaucluse. Enter **Cadenet** (98km ♣), where the 14/17C church has an attractive square 16C bell-tower and interesting font. Cross over the railway and keep following LOURMARIN, APT. The centre of **Lourmarin** (■ⓘ) is by-passed. (If you turn left into this lovely village, seek out not only the 15/16C château, but the cemetery where

Bories near Gordes. Some 3000 years of history unfold at the Village des Bories, an outdoor museum of rural life. Bories are thought to date from the Bronze Age (while their exact origin is unknown, they resemble dry-stone dwellings as far afield as Ireland, Sardinia, the Balearics and Peru). Bories were inhabited until the 18th century.

Albert Camus is buried.) The vineyards, cherry orchards and stone houses around Lourmarin are particularly attractive; the limestone soil glints in the sun. Lourmarin is our next gateway into the Lubéron: from here we climb the Combe de Lourmarin, the wooded gorge of the Aigue-Brun River that splits the massif in two. To our left is the Petit Lubéron, renowned for its perched villages (Tour 4), to our right the Grand Lubéron, culminating in the peak of Mourre Nègre (1125m/3700ft).

After 6.5km turn left on the D36 for BONNIEUX. *Exactly 3km* along, watch for a tiny brown-painted signpost on the left: FORET DES CEDRES, and turn left uphill *just before* the signpost. Some 3km uphill pass a viewpoint to the right (📷); if you are lucky enough to be able to park, this is a superb picnic spot, from where there are tremendous, if hazy, views down over Lacoste (left) and Bonnieux, surrounded by vineyards. At the top of the climb the tar ends (118km), and the track ahead is closed to motor vehicles. This is the **Forêt des Cèdres** (*P*), and the aroma is enchanting. Walk 4 starts here, and we especially recommend Short walks 4-2 or 4-3.

Return to the D36 and go left towards Bonnieux, *but after just 300m turn right* on the D232 for SAIGNON (easily missed). This is another road with some bories, most on private property (one of them, some 2km along, has been converted into a 'bijou' residence). When you meet the D943 turn sharp right for LOURMARIN. Just 1.4km along turn sharp left on the D113. A slender 12CR tower, all that remains of the old priory of

St-Symphorien (photograph page 131), is seen straight ahead. Just past it, turn right for BUOUX, immediately coming to a Y-fork, where you bear left *(not sign-posted)*. At the next junction, where a sharp left leads to Apt, go straight ahead for LES SEGUINS, FORT DE BUOUX. Take the road up right to the substantial remains shown on page 81, the **Fort de Buoux** (🏛 destroyed in the 17c by Louis XIV). When you return from the fort, head right for 300-400m to park for Walk 3.

Then go back to the U-turn of the D113 (about 0.6km back from the road to the fort) and bear right. Climb steeply below more impressive rock walls draped with ivy. Beyond **Buoux** an incredibly beautiful small valley opens up on the right (📷), then you cross over the D232 (📷 towards Apt). We are taking you into Apt and then out again immediately to give you the best view of Saignon. Curl down through orchards and meet a T-junction on the edge of **Apt**: turn right for DIGNE, SISTERON. Keep straight ahead at the lights and then, at a big roundabout (where the N100 crosses), *immediately take the first right turn*, the D48 for SAIGNON.

You climb past ugly flats but, after another kilometre, there are fine views★ (📷) over to Saignon on the left, huddled below 'mushroom-stalks' of striated rock. Stay on the D48, following AURIBEAU, CASTELLET; you turn right in front of **Saignon**, without entering the centre. At the next fork (where the D232 goes right to Bonnieux) go left. There is another superb view back to Saignon, focussing on the 12/16c church, as you climb above it on the D48. The road, hedged in by box and stone walls, now heads straight towards the Mourre Nègre. A few farmhouses with vineyards and herb gardens line the valley of the Aigue-Brun on the right. Approach the lovely hamlet of **Auribeau** but, just before reaching the church, turn left on the D48 to CASTELLET. Snake downhill with the Lubéron just on your right; on the left there are fine views towards St-Martin-de-Castillon on the far side of the Calavon Valley. Weave through **Castellet**, where burgundy-red roses spill out over stone walls. You pass the hamlet's rusty old lavender still as you leave.

Beyond Castellet turn left at a fork, cross the Calavon, and come to the N100. Turn left through gentle cultivation, grapes and crops. Enter **Apt** by ① and leave by ③, the N100 for AVIGNON and CAVAILLON. A few kilometres outside Apt turn right on the D4 for MURS, ROUS-SILLON. Then take a left back into **Roussillon** (166km).

Tour 3: MONT VENTOUX AND THE DENTELLES DE MONTMIRAIL

Roussillon • Sault • Mont Ventoux • Vaison-la-Romaine • Gigondas • Dentelles de Montmirail • Bédoin • l'Isle-sur-la-Sorgue (or Gorges de la Nesque • Roussillon)

182km/113mi; about 6-7h driving; Michelin map 81 or 245

En route: ⊞ at Vacqueyras; P on the northern flanks of Ventoux, Notre-Dame-du-Groseau, Col du Cayron, Roussillon; Walks 1, 5

Make an effort to get to Ventoux as early in the morning as possible; the heat haze builds up quickly, obscuring the wonderful views. The descent from Ventoux is a bit narrow at the start (unnerving for some drivers and passengers). No petrol from Sault to Malaucène (almost 50km on the tour). See the Alternative tour on page 29 if you wish to return to Roussillon via the Gorges de la Nesque. Consider breaking the tour into two days, staying overnight at Vaison-la-Romaine.

From the *table d'orientation* in Roussillon there is an enticing outlook towards Mont Ventoux rising almost due north. The summit, a sprawl of bare white limestone scree, looks snow-capped all year round. From a distance the mountain looks much higher than its 1909m/6262ft, because it rises in splendid isolation from the Carpentras and Vaucluse plains. And when you are on the summit, you will feel on top of the world — not only because of the panorama, but because of the bitter, icy-cold winds (*vents*) that buffet the peak. Take plenty of warm clothing, in case you want to venture out of the car! Be prepared for a drop in temperature of as much as 20°F (10°C), plus a high wind-chill factor. Later in the tour, you can stretch your legs in warmer surroundings, on the nearby Dentelles de Montmirail — the finely-etched 'lace' mountains.

Leave **Roussillon** on the D227 for ST-SATURNIN, MURS, APT. Cross straight over the D4 and after 8km turn right on the D2. At **St-Saturnin-lès-Apt** (⚓ and 15c gate) turn left on the D943 for SAULT, leaving the main part of the village off to the right. Travel through *garrigues,* with some fine views left over the plain, where red daubs reveal Roussillon with the Lubéron stretching out behind it. The road skirts the deep Urbane Valley on the left, as you approach the Plateau de Vaucluse. Pass to the right of the plane-shaded château of Javon (▮), just beside the road. This fortified building is in mint condition. Some 6km further on there is a fine view of Ventoux ahead beyond fields (see pages 28-29). Pass to the right of **St-Jean-de-Sault**, a pretty hamlet. Now Ventoux is in sight all the time, rising off the striped cultivation of the plateau, where lavender predominates.

Cross the Croc; Sault rises straight ahead on a rocky outcrop. Keep following SAULT and MONT VENTOUX, to go straight through **Sault** (♣M**i** and last ☕ for 50km), where there is a pleasant view from the terrace of the 12/14CR/G church and a small museum of Gallo-Roman antiquities. Sault is an important centre on the 'Route de la Lavande'. Like the 'Route du Vin', this is a recent marketing ploy, but a fairly well-defined swathe of blue and purple *does* extend across the Vaucluse Plateau from Vaison-la-Romaine all the way to Castellane (see *South of France: The Alps to Aix*). The cultivation of lavender was begun in the early 1900s, in an attempt to slow the depopulation of this countryside; the crop adapted perfectly to the chalky soil.

At a Y-fork go left for MONT VENTOUX on the D164, crossing the Nesque. Some 6km out of Sault there is a fine view (📷) back to the left, down over Sault and the cereal and lavender fields on the plateau. You start to climb through a beautiful mixed forest. In June the plumes of yellow-flowering laburnum light up the lower slopes. Two forks are met on the ascent: go left at both of them, although there is no signposting. Pass **Le Chalet-Reynard** (☕) on your right and go straight ahead.

Almost effortlessly, this excellent road takes you to the summit of **Mont Ventoux★** (65km), where the *table d'orientation* is split in two halves. First come to the southern viewpoint (📷☕), with an outlook stretching over your base in the Lubéron and as far as the Pyrenees. Then pass the relay station with its souvenir shop and chapel and descend to the northerly viewpoint, from where you can look out to the Alps and the coast by Nice.

From this viewpoint follow MALAUCENE, descending the north side of the mountain in hairpin bends. The road is quite narrow in places and not built up at the side. On the first U-bend, just to

Approaching Mont Ventoux on the D943; the streaky clouds herald the mistral.

the left of the observatory, there is another fine view of the Pyrenees. At the 'Ponts et Chaussées' building, go left for MALAUCÈNE, to keep on the D974. Soon pull up on the right at a viewpoint (📷) over the Dentelles. All the way down this side of the mountain there are gorgeous places under pines or cypresses (*P*), for picnics on *very hot days*! A better spot is Notre-Dame-du-Groseau, on your left after 85km (✝*P*); see description on page 9.

At **Malaucène** (✝ⓘ☕), where the 14c church is built into the ramparts, take the D938 northwest, to enter **Vaison-la-Romaine★** (95km 🏛✝Mⓘ) by ②. This exquisite small town rose above the Ouvèze as a Celtic *oppidum*, but came under Roman control in the 2nd century BC. If nothing else, visit the extensive Roman ruins. An overnight stop would enable you to to take in the other sights, as well as the excavations museum.

Leave Vaison by ③, the D977 (AVIGNON road). After some 5km turn left on the D88 for SÉGURET, with a wonderful view of the Dentelles straight ahead. Pass below **Séguret**, where the ruined castle rises up on the left, and turn right on the D23 for SABLET. Soon mellow **Sablet** is a pyramid in front of you, with its church at the apex; go left for GIGONDAS on the D7 just in front of the village. Keep left at all forks until you come into **Gigondas**, famous for its red Grenache wine. Here go left and left again for LES FLORETS. The lovely road climbs

Vineyards near the Col du Cayron at the Dentelles de Montmirail; if you turn left at the col, you can park below the Chapelle St-Christophe and picnic in the setting shown on page 7.

through vineyards towards the **Dentelles de Montmirail★**. Continue beyond the end of the tarmac; 0.7km of rough track takes you to the **Col du Cayron** (113km *P*), at the foot of the Dentelles Sarrasines, the most northerly of the two chains and the 'lacier'. Walk 5 starts here and takes you up, over and round the crests.

Return the way you came and keep following VACQUEYRAS, passing several *dégustations* and 🛱. Go straight through **Vacqueyras** on the D8. Following CARPENTRAS, continue south past the lovely R bell-tower of Notre-Dame-d'Aubune (🛉), then fork left on the D81 for BEAUMES. At the T-junction turn left into **Beaumes-de-Venise** (🍷) and, just beyond the church, turn left on the D90 for LAFARE. You pass a pretty chapel on the right. In **Lafare** continue straight ahead for SUZETTE. Along this stretch there are several good viewpoints back to the Dentelles (📷); the best is a large layby on the right just past the turn-off left to Châteauneuf. From here you can see the two parallel ridges side-on. From this angle the Grand Montmirail (on the left) looks just as razor-sharp as the Dentelles Sarrasines. This view is at its best early in the day, but makes a dramatic afternoon silhouette.

Go through **Suzette** and turn left for MALAUCENE. Some 4km along come to the Col de la Chaîne (📷; '472m' on the Michelin map). From here there is another superb side-on view back to the Dentelles and ahead to the lower flanks of Ventoux. Descend across a many-hued palette of cultivation, heading straight for Ventoux. Back in **Malaucène** (139km) follow TOUTES DIRECTIONS, almost straight ahead. Continue through the plane-shaded esplanade and then keep straight ahead on the D938 for BEDOIN and CARPENTRAS (where Ventoux is sign-posted to the left). Watch for your turn-off to Bédoin, 3km outside Malaucène; it is *not signposted,* but you must go left on the D19 beside poplars and cherry trees (a signpost appears on the left about a kilometre along!). Beyond a small lake on the right, climb past box hedges and umbrella pines to a grassy moorland

and the **Belvédère du Paty** on the right (📷); from here you look out over the plain, with the Lubéron (left) and the Alpilles (right) in the distance. Ventoux is ahead and to the left. Below, at picturesque Crillon-le-Brave, the clay quarries exude ochre hues. **Bédoin** (151.5km 🚶ℹ️), a gorgeous small perched village, has an 18cc church.

From Bédoin the main tour heads south to l'Isle-sur-la-Sorgue.* Follow CARPENTRAS through the village, heading south on the D974, passing the large Ventoux wine co-operative. Ignore the left turn for Mormoiron but, 5.5km from Bédoin, go left for MAZAN. In **Mazan** (🚶ℹ️) turn left following signposting for the tourist office, then turn right for PERNES. (Or first stop to visit the 12c church, where there is a wall built from 62 sarcophagi which once lined the Roman road between Sault and Carpentras.) Climbing out of the Auzon Valley on the D1, pull over to enjoy fine views back to the Dentelles, Ventoux, and east to the Montagne de Lure.

Continue over the D4, following PERNES. Cross the Canal de Carpentras and enter **Pernes-les-Fontaines** (172km 🚶ℹ️). At the traffic lights turn left for L'ISLE-SUR-LA-SORGUE and CAVAILLON (or keep straight ahead and take the *next* left, to visit this charming small town with its many fountains, 11c church and 16c gate, bridge and chapel). Once over the Nesque, the D938 quickly takes you to **l'Isle-sur-la-Sorgue★** (182km 17cc🚶 and ℹ️), one of our favourite towns, on account of the beautiful teal-green Sorgue River, the plane tree avenues, and the lovely old water wheels. There were once 10 wheels in this pulsating mill town.

*Alternative route back to Roussillon via the Gorges de la Nesque
Continue through Bédoin on the D19; outside the village, ignore the D974 climbing Ventoux from the south; keep on the D19 to **Flassan**, an ochre-coloured village. Leave Flassan on the D19 for VILLES-SUR-AUZON. In **Villes** *carefully* follow SAULT PAR ROUTE TOURISTIQUE, GORGES DE LA NESQUE (D942). The attractive *but sometimes narrow* road travels through holm oaks and manicured box hedges (🌲) above the deep Nesque Valley on the right. Fold after fold of mountain creeps out of hiding in the gorge ahead. About 12km from Villes you look towards the most impressive part of the gorge, where high vertical grey-rock walls rise sheer from the river. From now on there is a good run of *belvédères* (📷); the best are after the first and second of the exquisitely-sculpted tunnels — you look across to the massive abutment of the Rocher du Cire and up the gorge towards Mont Ventoux. Beyond here the gorge flattens out into the verdant swathe of the Nesque Valley. Pass below a 12c tower at **Monnieux** and keep right for SAULT, crossing the plateau, a tapestry of lavender and cereals. On meeting the D1 left to Villes, head right into **Sault**; then follow ST-SATURNIN, to return to **Roussillon** on your outgoing route (231km).

Tour 4: THE THREE-STAR ROUTE

L'Isle-sur-la-Sorgue • Fontaine-de-Vaucluse • Oppède-le-Vieux • Bonnieux • Avignon • Pont du Gard

124km/77mi; about 4h driving; Michelin map 81 or 245

En route: 🚉 at Tête du Soldat; **P** at Pont Julien, Pont du Gard; Walk 6 (Walks 3 and 4 are nearby)

The ideal way to do this tour is to set out no later than 8am, to be at the Fontaine de Vaucluse before the crowds. Leave there by 9am and potter about the Lubéron (or do Walk 3 or 4), getting to Avignon late in the day, to break the tour. Spend the next day at Avignon and arrive at the Pont du Gard in the early evening. If you have only one day, you can still see the highlights of Avignon during the afternoon. Note that at peak times the Pont du Gard is open one-way only — from north to south. So if you are staying at one of the hotels on the north side (Rive Gauche), you may prefer to follow RIVE GAUCHE *outside Remoulins; there is a small parking area on the north side.*

This short tour takes in not only the most popular tourist attractions in Provence, but some of the finest perched villages in the Lubéron. *Do* set out early, to have these landscapes (almost) to yourself.

From **L'Isle-sur-la-Sorgue** take the D938 north (CAR-PENTRAS, FONTAINE-DE-VAUCLUSE) through a double avenue of planes. Cross the Sorgue and turn right on the D25, following FONTAINE-DE-VAUCLUSE. Pass under an aqueduct and approach **Fontaine-de-Vaucluse★** (7km ✝🏛M🛈). Coming into the main square, turn left to the signposted parking area, just as you approach the central column, dedicated to Petrarch. Now set off on foot to the famous source: from the column take the tarmac lane at the left of the 'Snack Bar/Glacier'. You enter a magnificent *cirque*, below which the Sorgue rushes by on your right. After a climb of 15-20 minutes the path ends at a chaos of gigantic boulders. In summer or autumn all you will see is a tiny pool of murky turquoise water. It is hard to believe that this is one of the most powerful springs in the world! But in winter, when the vast underground reservoir in the bowels of the Vaucluse Plateau is full of rainwater, it's a different story — a deluge of emerald green water roars *over* the boulders.

Linger a while beside the rushing river, where Petrarch sought peace of mind and inspiration. When the first day-trippers snake into view, walk back to the village and take a look at the 11CR church, the old water wheel, and the derelict mills. Leave Fontaine-de-Vaucluse by following TOUTES DIRECTIONS from the square. Cross the Sorgue, then follow AUTRES DIRECTIONS until you can turn left for GORDES PAR ROUTE TOURISTIQUE (this is the narrow D100A, with a good view back left to the *cirque*

30

above the source). Ignore the turn-off right to Lagnes; continue left for CABRIERES. Soon come to the Belvédère du Tête du Soldat on the right (), overlooking Lagnes just below, the Alpilles and the Lubéron. Further on you pass a monument to the Resistance (), from where a footpath leads east to Cabrières and the 'Mur de la Peste' (see footnote page 77). At the next fork turn left, to squeeze through lovely **Cabrières-d'Avignon**.

From here to Oppède, care is needed to follow the convoluted roads. Go right and right again *immediately* (*not signposted; where a left turn goes to Gordes*). The Lubéron stretches straight in front of you now. At a Y-fork go right for COUSTELLET, passing a shrine on the left. Cross the D15 and meet the D2, where you turn right; the Lavender Museum is on your left here. Go straight over the N100 and, 11.5km further on, turn left on the D144 for MAUBEC and MENERBES. Just 0.4km further on, go left on the D3 (MENERBES, BONNIEUX, OPPEDE). On the right, vineyards spread out below the Petit Lubéron. Be sure to turn right, 1.5km further on, for OPPEDE-LE-VIEUX (D176). Then, after just 0.3km, bear right at a Y-fork (*easily missed*). Cross the D29 and go straight over for OPPEDE-LE-VIEUX; ignore the left turn to the village of Oppède.

Walking to the Fontaine de Vaucluse, we pass this ruined 13c castle and three museums: 'Le Monde Souterrain' (Vaucluse speleology), a Resistance museum, and a mill where paper is still made by traditional methods (fine viewing platform over the Sorgue).

Pont Bénézet — the famed 'Pont d'Avignon' of song. It was built in the late 12c by volunteers; legend has it that they were inspired by a young shepherd called Bénézet (later canonised). Of the original 22 arches, only four remain. The little Chapel of St Nicholas stands on one of the piers, a Gothic structure on Romanesque foundations.

As you approach **Oppède-le-Vieux★** (21km 🚶🏛️📷), pull over to the right for a dramatic view up to the ruined 15/16c castle and the church, with the houses fanning out below. Leave your car in the car park on the right and climb through the old gateway to the upper village. From both the castle and the church (13c, but twice rebuilt) there are fine views.

When you leave the car park turn right downhill. At a Y-fork go left for MENERBES and, 1km further on, go right for MENERBES at a roundabout. Ahead to the right are impressive limestone quarries. Then Ménerbes rises dramatically before you, spread along a ridge. Curve round in a U-turn below the village and, at the stop sign, go right for MENERBES, BONNIEUX. Come to a crossroads 0.6km further on and go left for Ménerbes CENTRE and LACOSTE. Climb through **Ménerbes★** (🚶🏛️📷) and fork left, following EGLISE, MAIRIE. When you come to the 14c church, pull over right to a viewpoint encompassing the plain, Gordes, Roussillon, the Plateau de Vaucluse, and Mont Ventoux. There is a Y-fork here: go right. Zigzag down to a road and turn right, then go sharp right again almost immediately. This is the D103 and, *after* you have turned, you will see a signpost for LACOSTE. Ignore the D218 left to Lumières, go straight ahead (signposted MENERBES!), then take the *next* left, the D109, for LACOSTE. Cross the river and pass the road to the Abbaye St-Hilaire on the right. The road runs through *garrigues* now, and you look straight ahead to the Mourre Nègre on the Grand Lubéron, with its relay station. Come into **Lacoste** (🚶📷), where the ruined château of the infamous Marquis de Sade and his family rises on the left. From here there is a fantastic view over the colourfully-cultivated patchwork of the Bonnieux plain straight ahead. Just 0.3km after entering Lacoste turn right on the D106 for BONNIEUX, leaving the centre of Lacoste off to your left. (There is a good view back to the 17c church from this turn-off). Some 2km further on turn left on the D109 for BONNIEUX, which rises ahead in a pyramid, with the church at the apex (⌖). Busy **Bonnieux★** (46km ✝☐ℹ⌖ and bakery M), the last of the perched villages en route, also boasts superb views — from the terrace in the centre, near the 12c church.

Leave Bonnieux for GOULT.* Keep following GOULT but, 3.5km from Bonnieux (just past a round dovecot on the right) turn right on the D108 for ROUSSILLON, APT. Then take the first left, go under the railway bridge, and turn left again immediately, to park at the **Pont Julien★** (**⊓**P). The three arches of this graceful 1c bridge supported the Via Domitia on its way south from Sisteron and Apt. Cross the bridge and meet the N100; turn left.

From here we will take the N100 almost all the way to the Pont du Gard. Keep following ISLE-SUR-LA-SORGUE and, from there, AVIGNON. As you approach **Le Thor** (13CR✝ with G vaulting) head left just before the centre, passing the splendidly extravagant bell-cage over the village gate. Then follow a lovely avenue of planes for the next 3km. (From here a detour of 6km return can be made to see the fine stalactites in the Grotte de Thouzon: head north from Le Thor on the D16.)

Enter **Avignon★** (94km ✝🖾Mℹ⌖) by ③. Here you leave the cradle of the Durance for the mighty Rhône. You will need a full day to see Avignon; if you are on a tight schedule, just climb the Rocher des Doms (viewing table). From there you can take in the ramparts, palaces, churches and bridges in one fell swoop — to say nothing of the surrounding and far-off countryside.

Leave Avignon by ⑥, taking the N100 for REMOULINS. Where the D976 comes in from the right (after 14km) turn left for REMOULINS. Pass under the motorway and go through **Remoulins** (120km). Now follow PONT DU GARD, RIVE DROITE, to the parking area on the right bank of the **Pont du Gard★** (124km **⊓**ℹP; notes and photograph pages 46-47). If you arrive late in the day, the crowds will have gone. The memory of an evening picnic on the river bank, as the sun sets, will stay with you forever.

*Or, to get to Walk 3 or 4, head south from Bonnieux on the D36 for LOURMARIN. After 1.5km you can turn right for Walk 4 (follow FORET DES CEDRES). To get to Walk 3, continue south for another 3.5km, then turn left for APT on the D943. After 2km go right for BUOUX (D113).

Tour 5: ANTIQUITIES AND THE ALPILLES

Pont du Gard • Nîmes • Tarascon • Les Baux-de-Provence • St-Rémy-de-Provence • Glanum • (Avignon) • Villeneuve-lès-Avignon • (Orange) • Pont du Gard

198km/123mi; about 6-7h driving; Michelin maps 80 and 84, or 245

En route: ⊼ on the D3 near Collias; **P** at Le Destet, D24 from Le Destet to Eygalières, St-Sixte, St-Rémy, Pont du Gard; Walks 6, 7, 8

Good, but busy roads. To visit Nîmes and just touch on nearby Avignon or Orange, you will need at least two days. If you plan to do the tour in one day and walk as well, save Nîmes (a nightmare of roundabouts) for another day and take this pretty route: at the 21km-point turn left on the D135 and keep on it via Poulx and Marguerittes to the D999. Pick up the tour again on the approach to Beaucaire.

This tour captures the essence of Provence, its history, landscape and flavour. Apart from seeing many of the most impressive Roman remains in the country, we visit Glanum, settled as early as 500BC but then overrun by the Barbarians, and Les Baux, court of the troubadours. Plane tree avenues and flat market gardens, hedged in by graceful windbreaks, provide the perfect foil for the glaring-white limestone massif of the Alpilles. Leave the car and every footstep crushes out a new heady aroma. *Ah! Ça sent la Provence!*

Referring to map 80, leave from the *left* bank of the **Pont du Gard** (the north side of the bridge), taking the D981 northwest towards Uzès. After 3.5km go left on the D112 for COLLIAS, through vineyards and orchards. Under 2.5km along turn left on the D3, still following COLLIAS and passing a pleasant grove of poplars (⊼). Cross the Alzon; on the right there is a lovely weir. At a fork in **Collias**, turn right on the D112 for SANILHAC. Beyond a car dump, notice the menhir on the left. In spring the young leaves of the cherry trees glow rosyred in the morning sun. On meeting the D979 go left for NIMES and PONT ST-NICHOLAS. You cross the Gard on a very narrow, wiggly nine-arch bridge (13c) at **Pont St-Nicholas**, a delightful hamlet. Once over it, go left; with luck you will find space to tuck in just beyond the bridge, to admire the setting and the gorgeous green

Les Baux-de-Provence, with the ruined castle at the far left. In the 13th century this fortified town was renowned as a court of love and visited by the troubadours. But in the 14th century it was in the hands of Raymond de Turenne — viscount by birth, but kidnapper by trade. When no payment was forthcoming, his victims were hurled from the castle into an abyss — to his great glee, by all accounts.

This triumphal arch south of St-Rémy, one of the finest Roman monuments in France, stood at the gateway to Glanum on the Via Domitia to Arles.

river. Then go through the Gorges du Gardon. *(Now, to avoid Nîmes, at 21km turn left for Poulx on the D135.)*

There is *no* proper signposting as you near Nîmes: on coming to a Y-fork, go left, following a small orange signpost, VILLE ACTIVE. Pass under the railway and enter **Nîmes★** (32km **IT■M🅸**) by ①. Park off Avenue Jean Jaurès, south of the Jardin de la Fontaine. First walk through these exquisite 18c gardens, with their fountains (in Roman times fed by water from the Pont du Gard) and the Temple de Diane. Then make for the Tour Magne on Mont Cavalier, the highest point in the city and the most impressive remains of the ancient fortifications. From the top, you can survey where you are going next — the white limestone Alpilles. Ventoux is seen in the north. When you descend from the tower, walk along Boulevard Victor Hugo, stop at the tourist office on your left, and then take in the two principal sights of Nîmes, the Maison Carrée and the arena.

Leave Nîmes by ③, the D999, and keep following BEAUCAIRE, TARASCON at all the roundabouts. This good road, often lined with planes, brings us into **Beaucaire★** (55km **■M🅸**) by ⑤. We cross the Canal du Rhône à Sète and then turn left, with the canal on our left — a very attractive setting. *Now, if you wish to stop here, quick action is called for!* Cross the canal a second time and, at the roundabout, take the fourth exit (CENTRE VILLE). Then *turn left again immediately,* to park on the plane-shaded quay, by the tourist office. You may wish to see the remains of the 11/13c castle (📷), which houses a museum of local history, including documents about the famous Beaucaire Fair. In medieval times as many as 300,000 people took part in these festivities in the course of one week. The fair was launched in 1217 by Raymond VI, Count of Toulouse (who figures prominently in the history of the Cathars; see box page 63).

If you are not stopping at Beaucaire, after crossing the canal a second time go straight on over the Rhône to the twin city of **Tarascon★** (**🕆■🅸**). The approach is magnificent: the seven towers of the massive château, one of the finest medieval castles (13/15c) in France, rise majestically above the wide, fast-flowing river. Almost adjacent to the bridge is the 9/14c church of Ste-Marthe, which was greatly damaged during Allied air attacks on bridges over the Rhône. After driving over the bridge, follow TOUTES DIRECTIONS through a long plane-shaded *place*. From here signposting for ST-REMY will take you out of Tarascon by ②, the D99.

Soon you can see the Alpilles ahead — slightly to the right. At a roundabout where the N570 crosses, go straight ahead. Almost at once you come into one of those fantastic plane-tree avenues which characterise this tour. Together with reeds and cypresses, they protect the market gardens here from the mistral. *Watch for the sign* denoting the exit from **Mas-Blanc-des-Alpilles** and, just 0.4km beyond it, turn right on the D31 (*not signposted; if you miss this road, turn right on the D27, which comes up shortly after*). Just over 2km further on turn right again, on the D27 (*not signposted*). Soon climb through aromatic pines and *maquis*. Just over 4km after joining the D27, watch for a tarmac lane off right (A26A); *immediately* beyond it turn *left* on another narrow lane (A38). After 0.6km turn up left to a *table d'orientation*★ (🔭), for breathtaking views over Les Baux and to the Camargue, the Rhône Valley, the Lubéron and Mont Ventoux. Short walk 8-2 starts here. Then return to the D27 and turn left.

As you approach **Les Baux-de-Provence**★ (76km ▯**M🛈**), park at the entrance to the village. Although at the heart of the Alpilles, Les Baux rises on a completely detached spur, with sheer escarpments on all sides; the site is extraordinary. Sadly but inevitably, today the village (photograph pages 34-35) is so commercialised that there is no enjoyment jostling through the alley-ways and ruins. If you are staying nearby overnight, try to get here first thing in the morning, although you will not be let into the ancient citadel until the gates open. Walk 8 comes into the village via some of the old bauxite mines, which were opened in the early 1820s and gave rise to the modern aluminium industry.

Leave Les Baux by turning left from the car park and then left again (D27). At the bottom of the hill again turn left, to **Maussane-les-Alpilles**. This is olive country (photograph page 74), and Walk 7 would plunge you into the sizzling groves. *Referring now to map 84,* take the D17 (MOURIES) left out of Maussane.* Then take the third left off the D17, the D78 to LE DESTET — one of the prettiest roads in Provence. The flat road skirts to the south of the crumpled white limestone **Chaîne des Alpilles★**. Espaliered fruit trees, olive groves, vineyards and the occasional flock of sheep in the road add character and colour to this thirsty landscape. Pass the Mas de Gourgonnier on the left, surrounded by vineyards and olive groves and then take the next left turn to **Le Destet**. *(Or, if you are going to do Walk 7 or have a picnic, continue past the Destet turn-off for 200m, then turn left on the next track you come to, where there is a wide irrigation channel ahead to the right.)*

From Le Destet follow the D24 towards EYGALIERES, a gorgeous pine-shaded road (**P**), bright with broom in spring, with views of the Alpilles to the left. Descending out of the pines, then enjoy lovely views of the foothills, with vineyards in front (photograph pages 92-93). At the junction with the D25 turn left for EYGALIERES, keeping on the D24. You head straight for the Alpilles, passing several *domaines*. Beyond the Vallonge vineyards, turn right for EYGALIERES on the D24B. **Eygalières** (97.5km), once a Neolithic settlement, now rises in terraces on a hilltop at the left of the road. Bear right to keep on D24B; a sign reminds you that the Resistance fighter Jean Moulin sheltered near here in January 1942. Turn off right to the 12C **Chapelle St-Sixte** (**✝P**; photograph pages 8-9), crowning a low hill.

Continue east from the chapel along the same road, flanked by beautiful Provençal farms and fields, with mountains rising in the far distance. Take the next left, a narrow lane *inconspicuously* signposted to VALDITION. Pass the entrance to this *domaine* and cross the Canal des Alpilles. The bamboo and cypresses used as windbreaks here are a delight. Go straight over the D73E and, when you meet the main road (D99), turn left. Soon planes arch over the road — the same shady cathedral of trees that you first entered at Mas-Blanc-des-Alpilles some 15km to the west! Through the trees you look left across gentle farmlands, where row upon

Or, if you want to see Daudet's mill★ at Fontvieille, take this (18km return) detour now: use map 83 and go right on the D17 out of Maussane to Fontvieille, then go left on the D33 in the centre of the village. From the mill you may wish to continue west on the D17 to the 12C Chapelle Ste-Croix and the 12C Benedictine Abbaye de Montmajour★ (26km return). Return to Maussane to continue.

row of cypress and poplar windbreaks stand out darkly against the white-lace chalk of the Alpilles.

Just over 10km after joining the D99 turn left for ST-REMY, GLANUM. Although there is nothing of great architectural importance in St-Rémy, it merits a star for its atmosphere — all light and shade, the true flavour of Provence, with its plane-shaded squares, fountains and intriguing lanes. St-Rémy was founded after the destruction of Glanum, from which important archaeological finds reside in the museum at the Hôtel de Sade. Enter **St-Rémy-de-Provence★** (116km M**i**) by ②. You join a one-way system: keep following AUTRES DIRECTIONS until you see LES BAUX signposted, then go right on the D5, leaving St-Rémy by ③. You pass the tourist office on your left shortly after turning off.

If you plan to do Walk 8 or you would like to picnic by a lake, keep an eye open now for a turn-off right, *inconspicuously* signposted LE BARRAGE (***P***). It comes up just under 1km from where you turned off for Les Baux. Otherwise pull up on the right 0.5km beyond this turn-off, at **Les Antiques★** (**i**), a mausoleum and the triumphal arch shown on page 36 — the surviving remains of the wealthy Roman city of Glanum, which was overrun by the Barbarians in the 3rd century and abandoned. Just over the road are the **Glanum excavations★** (**i**) of the oldest civilised buildings in France, covering about five acres. The area is thought to have been first settled by Celtic-Ligurian peoples (Glanics) in the 6th century BC, at the site of a sacred spring. Later building was carried out by the Greeks and then the Romans.

Return from here to St-Rémy and follow AUTRE DIRECTIONS and then TARASCON, BEAUCAIRE (exit ①). When you rejoin the D99 turn left, back under the planes. *(Switch back to map 80 now.)* After 9km along the D99, at a roundabout, take the first exit, the N570 for AVIGNON. *(The third exit here leads to Arles after 13km.)* La Montagnette, a 'mini-Alpilles', is seen ahead. At **St-Martin** turn sharp left on the D970 for BEAUCAIRE, TARASCON then, *just 0.7km further on,* turn sharp left again on a slip road (D81 for BARBENTANE). You circle over the D970 and the railway, heading across **La Montagnette**, where pines and olives vie for space. As you climb in hairpins, an impressively-sited 19c pilgrimage abbey, St-Michel-de-Frigolet, rises out of nowhere. Hidden among the buildings are a simple 12c church and 11c chapel.

Follow BARBENTANE (D35E) from the abbey, but then

take the first left, the D81 for BOULBON. At a T-junction with the D35 turn right (*not* signposted, but Beaucaire and Tarascon are signposted to the left). Then, just over 2km along, turn left on the D402 (MEZOARGUES, VALLA-BREGUES) and cross the Rhône. This handy bridge in the middle of nowhere avoids Tarascon and Beaucaire and takes you to an equally handy road — the D2: turn right and skirt the river, with good views to Avignon.

The castellated walls of **Villeneuve-lès-Avignon★** (♣■ℹ︎🎞) once enclosed the summer residences of the cardinals of Avignon. Pass the bridge into Avignon (158km; *possible detour*) and go right at the traffic lights. The 13/14c Tour de Philippe le Bel is straight ahead. Beyond another traffic light, either pull up left to this tower, or take the *next* left into the centre to park. Visit the 14c monastery (Chartreuse du Val de Bénédiction) and Fort St-André with its impressive gate. Then climb the Tour de Philippe for some of the most beautiful views on the tour, as the low sun burns out over Avignon, the Rhône and the Pont Bénézet. Ventoux is visible in the north, and you can trace all of the day's route through the Alpilles and La Montagnette.

From Villeneuve continue north on the D980 (exit ⑦), following BAGNOLS and then ROQUEMAURE. Beyond **Sauveterre** planes and poplars protect the orchards and fields of cereals lining the road. At **Roquemaure**, pass the 13c church, go through the little square, then *attentively* follow REMOULINS, NIMES, to head south* on the D976. Quickly passing the chapel of St-Joseph, carry on through vineyards backed by low wrinkled limestone hills. At a roundabout go straight over the N580, following NIMES. The famous rosé *domaine*, Tavel, begins here, ending 5km further on. There is a viewing terrace (🎞) at Notre-Dame-de-Grâce, an almshouse on your right, built on the site of a Benedictine priory. Then pass to the right of pretty **Rochefort-du-Gard**.

Soon the landscape deteriorates into suburbia. Meet the N100 (186km) and go right for NIMES (motorway sign) and REMOULINS, PONT DU GARD. Crest a hill and enjoy an excellent view down the Gard Valley up towards Uzès. Go under the motorway and through **Remoulins**. From there follow PONT DU GARD, RIVE GAUCHE, after 3km turning left, back to the north side of the bridge (198km).

*Or go *north* on the D976 to Orange★ (🎭), 11km away, to see the the triumphal arch which once stood on the Via Agrippa to Arles and the best-preserved Roman theatre in existence.

Tour 6: THE CAMARGUE AND ARLES

Pont du Gard • Beaucaire • St-Gilles • Aigues-Mortes • Stes-Maries-de-la-Mer • Digue à la Mer • Plage de Piémanson • Arles • Pont du Gard

278km/172mi; about 8h driving; Michelin map 83 or 245

En route: *P* at the Plage de Piémanson; Walks 6, 9

This is a two-day tour: on day 1 see the Camargue (allowing two hours for Aigues-Mortes); then stay overnight in Arles, devoting the next day to its wealth of sights. Some roads in the Camargue are very narrow; be prepared, too, for cars in front to come to a halt without any warning (the occupants have spotted some birds). The only petrol stations en route in the Camargue are at Stes-Maries and Salin.

The Camargue, a vast plain, is the result of a remorseless battle waged over millions of years between the silt deposits in the Rhône Delta and the salty waters of the Mediterranean. Man imposed a fragile truce in the latter part of the 19th century, when the waters of the Rhône were channelled and a sea-wall built (Digue à la Mer). From the Camargue we follow the Grand Rhône north to Arles, the finest Roman city in Provence and a Mecca for van Gogh enthusiasts. Wander the alleys in the evening; with luck the lamplight will fall upon an Arlésienne in her red and white costume, her bell-clear voice singing one of Bizet's well-known themes.

Leave from the left bank of the **Pont du Gard** and go right for REMOULINS. From there follow BEAUCAIRE on the D986. Skirting the Rhône, there is a view to the enormous Barrage de Vallabrègues on the left. Enter **Beaucaire** by ⑥ (22km 🛈; Car tour 5) and follow ST-GILLES, to leave by ④. Outside **Bellegarde** the D38 skirts the Canal du Rhône, before taking you into **St-Gilles** (48km ✝🛈). The west front of the 11/12c abbey church is a master-

Rice paddies ('clos') are flooded between April and September; they make a chequerboard of glassy pools, framed by poplars.

Montcalm makes a pleasant picture in spring.

piece of medieval sculpture. St-Gilles was home to the powerful Counts of Toulouse, who built up a vast domain and led crusades to the Holy Land. But when Pope Innocent III's envoy was murdered at St-Gilles in 1208, blame fell upon the current count, Raymond VI. He was excommunicated and forced to mount another crusade — against the Cathars (see box page 63). As a humanist who had always tolerated the heretics, Raymond soon rebelled against these orders.

Follow STES-MARIES-DE-LA-MER to head southeast on the N572 but, soon after crossing the canal, fork right on the D179. The Ecluse de St-Gilles is the lock that controls the canal between the Petit Rhône and the Canal du Rhône à Sète. Now you're in Haut or 'upper' Camargue, where desalination and fresh-water irrigation from the Rhône allows the cultivation of numerous crops, including wheat, vines, and fruit. Beyond **La Fosse** rice paddies dominate the landscape — the chief crop in the region, since it can withstand slightly salty water. At **Mas des Iscles** the road bears left beside the Capettes Canal. At **Montcalm**, where there is a ruined 18c château, flowering fields paint bold colours onto this muted canvas in spring (see above). Having joined the D58, cross the Canal du Rhône à Sète and go right on the D46 to the 14c **Tour Carbonnière**, a watchtower on the old salt road (■🗗), from where you can look out over Aigues-Mortes and as far north as the Cévennes.

Return to the D58 and turn right into **Aigues-Mortes★** (81km 🛈). The fascinating — and gruesome — history of this 13c fortified town (when its population was almost four times what it is today and the sea was more easily accessible) will keep you spellbound. Visit the ramparts and the Constance Tower (■🗗), and imagine the pageantry in 1248, when St-Louis embarked on his crusades with 35,000 men in 1500 chartered ships!

From Aigues-Mortes return to Montcalm and head right, to keep on the D58. Some 5km further on, go right on the D38 for STES-MARIES. The history of **Stes-Maries-de-la-Mer** (110.5km; 12CR fortified ✝★ and 🛈) is steeped in legend, and for centuries it has been a place of pilgrimage, especially for gypsies. Modern-day travellers' encampments being no more appealing in Stes-Maries than anywhere else, we are always glad to move on.

From here travel back north on the D570; lime-green rice paddies glimmer along both sides of the road. At the **Pont-de-Gau Bird Sanctuary** you can see many of the nearly 400 different birds identified in the area. The **Camargue Natural Regional Park★** was created in 1970, partly to protect the delta from an undisciplined spread of low-grade tourist facilities; its Information Centre (ℹ) is beside the Ginès Lagoon. At 132km turn right on the D37 for SALIN-DE-GIRAUD, soon passing a platform for bird-watching on your right. Soon you are driving into a monochromatic landscape with no perceptible horizon; the mesmerising silvery-blue **Etang de Vaccarès** shimmers beside you. Most of this vast lagoon (the centre of the region's fishing industry and one of the most important bird habitats) lies within the confines of the Nature Reserve. (Do not confuse the Regional Park, encompassing the whole of the Camargue, with the *inaccessible* Nature Reserve now on your right; the reserve is indicated on the Michelin map with dotted lines.)

In **Villeneuve** (146km) take the D36B to the right, following ETANG DE VACCARES. The wide road, lined with plane trees, continues to skirt the lagoon. You can hope to see some of the famous horses and bulls here, and look out on the left for a small thatched house, built to withstand very strong winds — the traditional dwelling of the herdsman or *gardian*. Unmistakeable in their wide-brimmed black felt hats, these 'Camargue cowboys' astride white horses cut an impressive figure.

The headquarters of the Nature Reserve is located at **La Capellière** (ℹ). Just past **Le Paradis** come to crossroads: ignore the left turn for Salin; keep straight ahead on the C135 (not numbered on the map). After 4km you reach the **Digue à la Mer★**, where a sign warns that 4-wheel drive vehicles are prohibited, and *all* traffic is prohibited in wet weather. Continue ahead for 1.2km,

43

to a pumping station, where you can park for Walk 9. You *can* go about 4km further, to the Pont de la Comtesse, but walkers and cyclists will not appreciate it.

Return towards Le Paradis, but turn right just short of the hamlet on the D36c. Pass the chapel of St Bertrand on the left opposite the St Bertrand farm (cycle rentals, horse riding, snacks). Some 9km beyond Le Paradis go right on the D36 (🚌) for **Salin-de-Giraud** (182km ℹ), gateway to the salt marshes. Salt has been drawn from the sea here since antiquity; originally destined for the table, today's output is used in the chemical industry. Great piles of salt (*camelles*) stand beside the road, with massive Caterpillars chomping away at them (📷). At 192km, the tar ends at the wide sweep of the 25km-long **Plage de Piémanson**. You could continue by car on the compacted sand (***P***) for another 3km and then walk west to the Phare de Faraman.

From here return past the salt piles and, at the junction with the D36c, keep right on the D36 for LE SAMBUC, ARLES. This road is very busy; you no longer have the luxury of stopping in your tracks. Fruit trees, conifers, and the fine-leafed tamarisk tree proliferate on the left, but the shimmering rice paddies on the right again steal your attention. Pass through **Le Sambuc** and at **Mas de Pontèves** keep right, to continue north on the D36. When you meet the D570 turn right to enter **Arles★** by ④ (240km 🎫🏛⛪Ⓜℹ). We would need a whole page just to touch on the highlights of this magnificent city.

If you are saving Arles for another day, on reaching the D570 follow ARLES and at the next roundabout NIMES, then bear right on the D15A to FOURQUES. Just through **Fourques** head left on the main D15 for BEAUCAIRE, passing a large irrigation control station. Vineyards give way to attractive fields of barley, edged by poplar windbreaks. Enter **Beaucaire** (256km) in the one-way system, which funnels you right, beside the Canal du Rhône à Sète. At the roundabout follow NIMES, cross the canal and *immediately* turn left. Keep following NIMES until REMOULINS is signposted; you leave Beaucaire by ⑥. Take your outgoing route back to the **Pont du Gard** (278km).

Tour 7: LES GARRIGUES

Pont du Gard • Uzès • Anduze • (Grotte des Demoi-selles) • Pic St-Loup • St-Martin-de-Londres • Lodève

177km/110mi; about 4-5h driving; Michelin maps 80 and 83, or 240
En route: P at Laroque (⊞), Montcalmès; Walks 6, 10

This is a short tour on good roads. There is ample time to see Uzès and the Grotte des Demoiselles, or to do Walk 10.

This tour crosses *the* Garrigues, a limestone plateau stretching from the Gard to Hérault and forming a buffer between the mountains to the north and the vine-yards of the Mediterranean basin. It's an arid landscape, sun-baked and freckled with holm oaks and aromatic herbs. Suddenly two spectacular peaks erupt off the plain and break the monotony — St-Loup and Hortus. Les Garrigues were traditionally the domain of sheep, and Lodève was an important centre for the wool industry from the 13th century until the mid 1900s.

Start out by referring to Michelin map 80. Leave the **Pont du Gard** from the north (Rive Gauche) and turn left on the D981. Pass the picturesque Château de Castille and the village of St-Maximin, both on the right. After crossing the Alzon you soon see the towers of **Uzès★** rising ahead. The town (14km ♠⛪ℹ) dates from medie-val times. If you have time for a visit, highlights include the 11-16c Duché (ducal château) and the 12c Tour Fenestrelle, a six storey-high cylindrical bell-tower.

Leave Uzès by ③, the D982 for MOUSSAC, ANDUZE, ARPAILLARGUES. An avenue of plane trees welcomes you into pretty **Arpaillargues-et-Auriac**, with its old stone houses, flowering balconies and c church with lovely wrought-iron bell-cage. More planes take you out of Arpaillargues, then you pass Auriac off to the left. Once in a while a vineyard punctuates the fields of cereal crops lining both sides of the road. After crossing the Bourdic you enter another gorgeous avenue of planes.

Just outside **Garrigues** you have a first glimpse of *garrigues*. But the isolated patch of limestone scrubland introduced by this eponymous village quicky ends, and you come back into gentle agricultural land and plane tree avenues. Just before entering Moussac, go right on the D18 for BRIGNON. Beyond **Cruviers** the Gard is seen on the left. Ignore signs to Ners; follow ALES, to keep on the D18. When you meet the N106 turn left for NIMES, cross the Pont de Ners (with a lovely view right over the Gard), then *immediately* turn hard right on the D982 for ANDUZE. Crossing a plain, you look straight ahead to the distant Cévennes. Go straight over the N110. Beyond peach orchards and vineyards you come into **Atteuch**, the foothills of the Cévennes are just in front of you. Now cherry orchards take you below the 12c Château de Tornac on a hill to the left and towards **La Madeleine**. The Gardon d'Anduze is on your right.

Continue over the railway and follow an avenue of planes into **Anduze** (58km [i]). The village is beautifully sited below high cliffs at the Porte des Cévennes — a gorge where two tributaries of the Gard converge. If you are pressed for time, as you approach the pretty fountain in the main square, turn left *(not signposted)* for ST-HIPPOLYTE-DU-FORT (D133), keeping the Cévennes to your right. Otherwise, first take a break in the attractive square, with its c church and 14c clock tower. Beyond the 11CR church in **St-Félix-de-Pallières** you finally come into Les Garrigues — a scruffy landscape of holm oaks, acacias and pines. Enter **Monoblet** and curl down

The Pont du Gard, one of the most beautiful and impressive monuments in the world, is in almost perfect condition, marred only by the introduction of a road bridge in the 18th century. Completed in the 1st century, the aqueduct carried water from the Eure spring near Uzès to Nîmes — a distance of almost 50km. Where it spans the Gard, it is the highest watercourse the Romans ever built (49m/160ft). One could sit here all day musing upon the genius of the architects who varied the span and recessing of the arches, to make them both pleasing to the eye and flexible in the event of subsidence. Even the stones protruding from the surface served a dual purpose: they supported scaffolding during restoration work, while at the same time adding visual interest. But ponder too — and with a shudder — the scene at this ancient construction site, with slaves and goats manœuvering the massive blocks (some weighing as much as six tonnes) into position, then fixing the gigantic clamps used to hold everything together in the absence of mortar.

o the left in front of the clock tower. At **St-Hippolyte-du-Fort** follow CENTRE VILLE and cross the Vidourle. On coming to a plane-shaded square follow TOUTES DIRECTIONS by going left and then right. Ignore the right turn o Cros; go straight over for GANGES (D999).

The Montagne de la Séranne stretches out to the left on the approach to **Ganges** (90km ). This medieval own was a silk-weaving centre during the reign of Louis XIV and still has a busy textile industry. Avoid the centre by taking the third exit from the roundabout, ollowing MONTPELLIER on the D986. *(Change now to map 33.)* Slanting plane trees take you into **Laroque**, where an equally slanting church looks out over the Hérault on the right. The river tumbles over weirs (P) and oon rushes foaming into a dramatic gorge of steep, orange-hued striated rock. Kayaks add colour to this refreshing scene. (To visit the Grotte des Demoiselles★ urn up left 0.7km beyond the signpost indicating the

start of **St-Bauzille-de-Putois**. These spectacular caves hide-outs during the Wars of Religion and the Revolution, are best known for the 'Cathedral' and the colossal white stalagmite resembling the Virgin and Child.)

From the Col de la Cardonille there is a fine view left to a limestone ridge rising straight off the plain and culminating in the Pic St-Loup. Beyond the col take the first left, the D1 to **Notre-Dame-de-Londres** (✝▮). Follow CENTRE VILLE and ST-MATTHIEU through this flower-filled little village. Pass the wine cooperative on the left and look right to see the 12c castle and 11c church. The D1 curls down through oaks to **Pic St-Loup**, then continues east below the mountain. From this angle the stark rusty-coloured vertical face of Hortus, the mountain on the left, commands attention, while Pic St-Loup tails off on the right. On coming to a Y-fork where the D1E9 goes left to Valflaunès (117km), turn round and retrace the road. Heading west, St-Loup again dominates the landscape. The ruined château of Montferrand up to the left belonged to Raymond VI, but was taken from him during the wars against the Cathars (see box page 63).

Some 5km after turning back, go left on the D122 for ST-MARTIN-DE-LONDRES, through *garrigues* brightened by a blaze of poppies in spring. Come into **St-Martin-de-Londres** (128km ✝): pass a modern wine cooperative on the right and catch a glimpse of the very pretty 12c priory-church in the arcaded old town. Bear left, following MONTPELLIER, then go right on the D32 for VIOLS. (After 4.5km you pass the turn-off left to the Copper Age Village Préhistorique de Cambous★ ▮▮.) Beyond **Viols-le-Fort** you come to **Puéchabon** (143km). To park for Walk 10 (*P*), turn right in front of the large calvary at the far end of the village and go right again immediately.

Continue through **Aniane**; soon planes lead into **Gignac** (▮). From here follow LODEVE, to join the N109/E11 west. The road crosses the Hérault on the Pont de Gignac★. Pull up on the right, cross the road *carefully*, and take steps down to admire this lovely 18c bridge. At **St-André-de-Sangonis** be sure to follow LODEVE, to leave by the N109/E11. Beyond **St-Félix-de-Lodez** meet the N9/E11 and go right for LODEVE, soon zipping along the dual carriageway. Enter **Lodève★** (177km ✝▮) by ②. This city, a convenient touring base, is very old: Nero had coins minted here to pay for the upkeep of the Roman legions. The 13c St-Fulcran Cathedral, with its square tower, has an impressive interior.

Tour 8: CIRQUE DE NAVACELLES

Lodève • Gorges de l'Hérault • St-Guilhem-le-Désert • Brissac • Gorges de la Vis • Cirque de Navacelles • Le Caylar • La Couvertoirade • Lodève

180km/112mi; 7-8h driving; Michelin map 83 or 240

En route: *P* by the river Hérault or the Vis, municipal park at Brissac, *lavogne* at La Couvertoirade; Walks (10), 11

Some roads are narrow and winding. Some drivers and passengers may find the road down into Navacelles unnerving: it is quite narrow (route difficile on the Michelin map), but it is wide enough for two cars to pass and is built up at the side.

This tour follows the gorgeous green Hérault to St-Guilhem-le-Désert with its Romanesque abbey church. From this exquisite setting we continue north beside the river and then trace its foaming tributary, the Vis … to the Cirque de Navacelles — a landscape so astonishing that you will blink in wonder and disbelief.

From **Lodève** follow MILLAU, MONTPELLIER. Cross the Pont de la Bourse (No 4 on the Michelin plan) and, at the T-junction, go left for MILLAU. Pass an Esso station on the left and then turn right on the D153 for ST-PRIVAT. Climb through oaks and chestnuts, with glimpses of Lodève below on the right. Beyond rolling fields of cereals, descend in deep shade, passing the entrance to the priory of St-Michel-de-Grandmont (✝) on the right and coming upon vineyards. Soon a huddle of reddish-orange houses appears ahead — **St-Privat**; Les Salces sits beyond it, on the other side of the terraced valley.

Ignore the D144 right to Usclas; continue through **Les Salces** and turn left at the T-junction beyond it (VERS CD9). On meeting the D9 turn right for AR-BORAS, descending below the rocky crown of the Rocher des Vierges, with fine views right (📷) over an enormous tapestry of

Park at Brissac (P)

vineyards — the Vignoble de St-Saturnin. Squeeze through the honey-hued houses of **Arboras** and, just before the sign denoting the end of the village, pull up right to overlook these gorgeous vineyards again (📷).

Keep left at the Y-fork in the long village of **Montpeyroux**. Just after passing a second church, turn left on the D141 for ST-JEAN-DE-FOS and GIGNAC, then immediately go right in front of the wine co-operative (ℹ️). Just 0.5km further on bear left for ST-JEAN-DE-FOS, still on the D141. Go straight ahead into **St-Jean-de-Fos**; the road becomes the D4 and takes you through the village (keep left for ST-GUILHEM). Just over 1km outside St-Jean turn right on the D27 for ANIANE, GIGNAC. Cross a bridge and immediately turn right and park. From here there is a fine view to the 11c Pont du Diable★ spanning the Hérault on your right (*P*; photograph page 71).

Go back over the modern bridge to the D4, then turn right for ST-GUILHEM, following the **Gorges de l'Hérault★**. Almost at once pass the busy **Grotte de Clamouse★**. Soon the river is just beside you on the right, a brilliant emerald green with kayaks whizzing by. **St-Guilhem-le-Désert★** (36km 🍴) lay along the pilgrimage route to Santiago de Compostela (Chemin de St-Jacques). To visit the magnificent 11cR abbey church, turn left opposite the restaurant on the main road and then park. *(Walk 10 affords magnificent views over St-Guilhem's superb setting below the Cirque de l'Infernet; see page 102. It starts near Puéchabon, 10km away. To get there, go back past the Pont du Diable, cross the modern bridge, and head east on the D27E and D32.)*

Continue north on the D4; the gorge has flattened out, but the wide Hérault flows just beside the road (📷*P*). Beyond a weir the road turns away from the river. In the hamlet of

Cirque de Navacelles from the north. Nothing prepares you for this setting: a giant cavity, 300m/1000ft deep, lies beneath you, completely encircled by steep limestone walls. At the bottom sits a hamlet, smoke curling from the chimneys. Beside the hamlet, a 'moat' encircles a tiny hillock. The 'moat' and cirque were created from the original meander of the Vis; then the river cut across the ox-bow to race straight through, a turquoise-blue ribbon tumbling over a waterfall in its haste to escape through a narrow gorge. The overall impression is of a magnificent gem in a flawless setting ... the more so in spring, when the cereal crops in the moat positively shimmer green, like a well-cut emerald caught in strong light.

Causse-de-la-Selle follow BRISSAC and GANGES. Through the trees you can see the spine of the Montagne de la Séranne stretching out on the left. Some 7km beyond Causse-de-la-Selle you pass a 15c three-arched hump-back bridge on the right (**P**); beyond it stands the 15CR church of St-Etienne d'Issensac (✝). After enjoying a lovely vista of vineyards and pollarded trees, ignore the D108 right to the Grotte des Demoiselles★.

Brissac (62km ✝▉ℹ**P**) is a delight. From the village park (turn left just past the 12c church with its faïence-roofed tower) you have a good view of the 16c castle atop the hill. In **Cazilhac** look to the right, through planes, to glimpse the attractive stone houses in the old part of the village. Just beyond Cazilhac, do not cross the bridge on the right into Ganges; continue straight ahead on the D25, following CIRQUE DE NAVACELLES.

We leave the Hérault and follow the lower **Gorges de la Vis★** from Ganges to Madières. The Vis bounds along on our right, making its presence felt through the very wooded surrounds. Some 2.5km along there is parking and access to a swimming stretch, below a weir. Just past here, a derelict paper mill is passed at **La Papeterie**. As we climb, little hamlets with red tile rooftops keep popping out of hiding. One of them is

Madières (left) and the bright pink Menhir de la Trivalle (right)

Gorniès, where we cross the Vis. Magnificent conifers introduce **Le Grenouillet** (🏠), and vertical limestone cliffs tower overhead. At enchanting **Madières** (photograph above) you have a choice: you can go *right* for NAVACELLES, BLANDAS (the northern route to the *cirque*). We keep to the D25 (NAVACELLES, ST-MAURICE) to approach from the south.* Pass a small power station just below the road on the right and climb in deep hairpin bends. Just under 5km uphill from Madières, when you are almost at the top of the climb, turn off right into a large layby (📷), with magnificent views down the gorge. Over to the left is the plateau where you are heading.

At **St-Maurice-Navacelles** (93km) turn right on the D130 for CIRQUE DE NAVACELLES, crossing the **Causse du Larzac★**, a limestone plateau peppered with box, *Cistus*, asphodels, honeysuckle and wild flowers. On coming to a farm, La Baume-Auriol (98.5km 📷💺), park and walk to the edge of the plateau. From here there is a breathtaking view down over the astounding **Cirque de Navacelles★**. It is easy to see why this was one of the hideouts of the Maquis. Then continue past the farm, to descend (📷) to Navacelles. *Take the somewhat vertiginous descent slowly; you've only a short way to go.* On reaching a T-junction (where Walk 9 leaves the road to follow a path to the source of the Vis), go right into **Navacelles** (102km ⛰️✕; see also photograph pages 12-13). There is a lovely bridge here, a gorgeous waterfall, and a sprinkling of houses.

Return from the village to the junction, and go straight ahead (right) over the river (*P*) for BLANDAS, LE VIGAN. The D713 ascends the canyon, above the Vis (📷). At a layby 2.5km uphill, where you overlook a cedar wood, there is a *sentier botanique* down to the source of the

*We think this is by far the more dramatic approach. We then *return* via the north and Blandas, to take advantage of the brilliant descent overlooking Madières; this does have the slight disadvantage of repeating the 7km-long stretch between Madières and St-Maurice.

Vis and the setting shown on pages 104-105 (see dotted red line on the map on page 105). Another layby under 2km further on offers the view of the *cirque* shown on pages 50-51. (The GR7 ascends here from Navacelles; if you take a look at the path, you will see why we don't recommend *all* GR routes, although the climb would be less difficult than the descent!) After leaving the *cirque* and heading inland, turn right at a T-junction on the D158 for ROGUES. Under 3km from the T-junction, just before tiny **Rogues**, look out on your left for the Menhir de la Trivalle (photograph opposite). Some 0.3km further on, turn right for MADIERES on the D48 and pass through the attractive hamlet of **Le Cros**. The road, flanked by oaks, skirts a gorgeous valley on the right, eventually descending to superb views over Madières.

At the signpost introducing **Madières** go straight ahead for ST-MAURICE, crossing the Vis and retracing your route up the gorges. Back in **St-Maurice** (130km) cross over the D130 on the D25, following ST-PIERRE. This flat road zips straight across a plateau where barley is grown. A wrought-iron cross is passed on the left and then an attractive farm, the Mas-de-Jourdes. *(Not far past here you might like to turn left and pop in and out of La Vacquerie, just because it is such a pretty hamlet.)* Enter **St-Pierre-de-la-Fage** (139km) and turn right for LE CAYLAR (D9), again crossing the Causse du Larzac. Pull over right some 9km out of St-Pierre (📷), to admire the quilt of fields ahead, each patch edged by tall hedges of white-flowering ash — a magnificent sight in early summer. Not far past here you look ahead to the dolomitic rocks above Le Caylar, where there is a cross. If you stop at the tourist office in **Le Caylar** (152km ℹ), notice the carved elm in front. Go straight through this village with its old houses and clock-tower, following MILLAU on the N9. Over to the right, more fine examples of dolomitic rock spew out from Le Caylar. Just over 2.5km outside Le Caylar, approaching the motorway, turn right on the D55 to the beautifully-preserved 12/14c fortified village of **La Couvertoirade★** (159km ■ℹ). It belonged to the Knights Templar and was refortified by the Hospitaliers. Outside the village walls (turn right from the main gate) is a fine *lavogne* (**P**), suggesting that the knights kept sheep on the *causses*.

From here return to Le Caylar, join the motorway and, when it ends, continue on the N9/E11 back to **Lodève** (180km), entering at ①.

Tour 9: CASTLES IN THE AIR

Lodève • Cirque de Mourèze • Mons • Olargues • St-Pons-de-Thomières • Mazamet • Carcassonne

184km/114mi; 5-6h driving; Michelin map 83 or 240

En route: ⊼ on the D908 between Olargues and Riols, Plo de la Bise, D118 near Les Martys; *P* at the Lac du Salagou (⊼), Château de Malavieille, La Mouline, Cirque de Mourèze, Gorges d'Héric; Walks 12-18

This short tour leaves plenty of time for you to enjoy one of the superb walks en route — or, if you don't plan to do Car tour 10, to include the Pic de Nore (pick up Car tour 10 at the 138.5km-point). All the roads are good; some are busy.

We make for Carcassonne, our base at the end of this long tour through the South of France, and our gateway to the Pyrenees. Lofty castles, all different, provide the focal point. First there is a chance to climb to a ruined 12th-century château and inspect some nearby dinosaur footprints. Not long afterwards we come upon the limestone 'battlements' of the Cirque de Mourèze: while there *is* a real ruined castle here, what captures the imagination are the rock formations, which resemble ruined ramparts. Finally we reach Carcassonne — rising straight up from the plain, the old walled *cité* is a fairy-tale come to life.

From **Lodève** follow MILLAU, MONTPELLIER. Cross the Pont de la Bourse (4 on the Michelin plan). On the far side of the bridge, at the T-junction, go right for MONTPELLIER, LAC DU SALAGOU. This feeder road takes you to Exit ②, the N9/E11 dual carriageway south. After 7km bear right for OCTON on the D148. Round the north edge of the **Lac du Salagou** (*P*), a popular watersports centre. Three high hills jut into the lake, but seem to rise up out of it. Burgundy-red soil enhances this landscape, shown on pages 108-109. Pass to the left of Octon and bear left on the D148E for MAS DE CLERGUES. At a Y-fork 2km from Octon go straight ahead through vineyards for MERIFONS. Enter **Malavieille** 1.3km after turning off for Mérifons. Go straight through; 0.6km beyond the sign denoting the village boundary, you could park for Walk 12. Continue for another 1.6km, to the hamlet of **La Lieude**. Park on the right below the ruined Château de Malavieille (*P* and Short walk 12), by a large shelter housing the footprints of prehistoric animals (see notes on page 108).

The ancient bridge and bell-tower at Olargues

Return to the D148ᴇ and continue towards Salasc, crossing a river and coming upon La Mouline, the exquisite setting shown on page 57 (*P*). The Château of Malavieille is visible in the northwest. At lovely **Salasc** take the second left, the D8 for ᴍᴏᴜʀᴇᴢᴇ. Soon the **Cirque de Mourèze★** rises on your left, the wonderful 'wild west' setting for Walk 13 (*P*; photograph page 11). The French have a perfect word for this chaos of dolomitic rock — *ruiniforme:* the eroded formations resemble ruined monuments, buildings, or even villages. Although very touristic, **Mourèze** (28.5km 🕐) is beautifully kept. A ruined castle rises on vertical cliffs above the chaos; the ʀ church is much rebuilt.

Continue straight through the village. You pass a graveyard for fallen Maquisards on the left, just before meeting the D908. Turn right on this busy road and soon have a fine view of the Montagne de Liausson, rising behind vineyards. If you did Walk 13, you will know how easy it is — and how rewarding — to climb it. Pass to the left of the small industrial town of **Bédarieux** and turn left on the D909 for ʙᴇᴢɪᴇʀs, ᴘᴇᴢᴇɴᴀs. Cross the D146 and continue ahead for ʙᴇᴢɪᴇʀs. *(Just before entering a tunnel you can take a 3.5km return detour on the left to a table d'orientation atop Pic de Tantajo, for a panoramic view over the Orb Valley and surrounding countryside; the one-lane road is very narrow.)*

Go through the Tunnel du Col du Buis and turn right for ʜᴇʀᴇᴘɪᴀɴ on the D909ᴀ, driving under an attractive railway bridge and crossing the Orb. In the centre of

Hérépian (62km), at the roundabout, go left on the D908 for LAMALOU and ST-PONS. As you follow a beautiful plane-tree lined avenue, notice the lovely 12CR chapel of St-Pierre-de-Rhèdes (♣) in a cemetery on your right, just beyond the turn-off for Lamalou. Some 4km beyond **Le Pujol-sur-Orb** look left for a gorgeous view over the Orb Valley, where the fair fields and green-gold vineyards of a solitary *domaine* gird the darkly-wooded hillsides like an embroidered belt. In total contrast, the bare peaks of the Massif du Caroux now rise on the right. **Mons-la-Trivalle** (77km 🛈), near the confluence of the Jaur and Orb, is the starting point for Walk 14 in the Gorges d'Héric (*P*) — one of the most rewarding walks in the South of France.

A slender 11c bell-tower welcomes you into beautiful **Olargues★**. Beyond the railway bridge, you pass a road coming in from Le Cros on the right; Walk 15 descends it. Go through a pretty little gorge and, immediately after passing a Total petrol station on the right, turn left to a parking area (from where the photograph on pages 54-55 was taken). There is a fine view to the bell tower and the 12c Pont du Diable. Walk 15, a delightful and easy circuit above the village, starts here.

From Olargues follow the Jaur through a very wooded open gorge. Pass the large Aire de St-Vincent (🛏) on the left, in a basin overlooking the river. Then go through **La Canarie**, a large hamlet with lovely stone houses. As you near **Premian**, greenery cloaks the Espinouse mountains ahead of you like a sable coat. **Riols**, with its simple R church, straddles the road. On the approach to St-Pons, bear right on the N112. Come into **St-Pons-de-Thomières** (100km ♣M🛈; Car tour 10). As soon as you pass the cathedral on the right, pull up either to the left or right and park just before the roundabout (Place Forail). The excellent tourist office (where Walk 16 begins) is in the Maison du Pays.

From the roundabout continue west on the N112 for MAZAMET. Just beyond the D920 left to Carcassonne, you pass the obscurely-signposted turn-off right to the **Grotte de la Devèze**. Go through **Labastide-Rouairoux**, from where there is a gorgeous view left to the northern flanks of the Montagne Noire, smothered in trees. On the right the Monts de Lacune make a pleasant Alpine setting of rolling green hills. Beyond **St-Amans-Soult** (where the first of the churches has an octagonal tower), you approach Mazamet via the industrial outskirts. Pass

La Mouline, a gorgeous farm not far south of Octon

mills selling leather goods at 'factory prices' and, at the first roundabout, follow MAZAMET CENTRE, CARCASSONNE. You enter **Mazamet** (135km ✝M🛈; Car tour 10) by ①. Now follow TOUTES DIRECTIONS and then CARCASSONNE, to leave Mazamet by ②. But, if you would like to take a lovely walk here, full of history, then see the notes for Walk 17 on page 121. *(Or, if you are not walking, you might like to go to Carcassonne via the Pic de Nore. See page 60: follow Car tour 10 from Mazamet. This adds only 14km to the tour, but driving will be slower.)*

Climbing the D118, you reach the **Belvédère du Plo de la Bise** (🚗🎪 and seasonal 🛈), overlooking Mazamet and the colourful old red-roofed factories beside the bounding river Arnette (one of the settings for Walk 17). Pass the D1009 left to the Pic de Nore, then descend through rolling hills and farmlands (🎪). Beyond **Les Martys** you enjoy tantalizing glimpses of the Dure Valley on the right through conifers (🎪). Chestnut trees line the approach to **Cuxac-Cabardès**, and parcelled-up fields and vineyards blanket the rolling hills on the left.

The approach to Carcassonne is uninspiring; it betrays nothing of the magic about to begin. Follow CARCASSONNE at a first roundabout; the Canal du Midi (setting for Walk 18) is on your left. At next roundabout take the third exit (LA CITÉ), to enter **Carcassonne** (✝M🛈) by ①. Now signposting for La Cité disappears! Follow NARBONNE, to *leave* Carcassonne by ②. You head east on the N113: after 2km, just after the dual carriageway begins, turn right for LA CITÉ; this road takes you to the parking area at **La Cité★** (184km ✝🍴M🛈), the world's finest example of a medieval fortified town (see pages 58-59). The *only* way to see it is 'out of hours', so have dinner in the square and then wander the lamp-lit alleyways.

Tour 10: MONTAGNE NOIRE

Carcassonne • Citou • St-Pons-de-Thomières • Lac de la Raviège • Mazamet • Gorges de l'Arnette • Pic de Nore • Gorges de la Clamoux • Carcassonne

201km/125mi; 6-7h driving; Michelin map 83 or 235

En route: ♨ at the Col du Cabaretou, **P** at Roc Suzadou (♨), Trèbes (♨); Walks 16-18

All the roads are good, although some are quite narrow. Make sure you have enough petrol before crossing the Montagne Noire whether north- or southbound, and for the circuit of the Lac de la Raviège.

The Montagne Noire, the most southerly chain of the Massif Central, is the focal point for this tour. We move from the Minervois vineyards on its parched Mediterranean foothills to lush green highlands and magnificent forests of beech and firs. A brief foray into a more northerly range, the Espinouse, opens our way to the circuit of a lovely man-made lake. Most of the tour lies within the boundaries of the Parc Naturel Régional du Haut-Languedoc, created in 1973 to help these rural communities improve their quality of life, while at the same time preserving the environment and stemming depopulation. ('Green' tourism is encouraged, with 1800km of waymarked footpaths in the park.)

To leave **Carcassonne** by ①, first follow TOULOUSE and then MAZAMET. You join the D118, skirting the Canal du Midi on your right. After 0.6km, walkers could be deposited by the roadside to join Walk 18 at Pont Rouge (signposted), where they can cross the bridge to the towpath (see map pages 126-127). Just beyond here, at another roundabout, take the first exit (D620 for VILLALIER). Leave the built-up area behind; signs proudly proclaim that you are in the domain of the Minervois

vineyards and the land of the Cathars (see box page 63).

Keep right outside **Villalier**, following CAUNES. The gentle southern slopes of the Montagne Noire rise ahead. The public gardens at **Villegly** are a fine splash of greenery. At a fork with the D11 bear left for CAUNES, CITOU. Pass to the left of **Caunes-Minervois** (🌟), where the 7C Benedictine abbey was restored in the 1700s. Follow CITOU and, at the next fork, ST-PONS. The D620 skirts the wooded gorge of the Argent-Double with its rustic stone farmhouses. The Minervois is left behind, and you move from the Mediterranean foothills to the verdant north. This next stretch of the tour, from here to the N112, is the most beautiful. Notice the ruins of the château on the hill at **Citou** (31km 🗓) and then the pretty stream falling in tiers on the right. **Lespinassière** is a particularly attractive perched village (🗓📷), dominated by its restored 15C clock-tower. Go through the village with its lovely old buildings and when you've climbed out of it, stop as soon as you clear the trees; there is a magnificent view back over the village and tower (just beyond a metal bench on the right). Two kilometres further on pass a sign commemorating Resistance fighters, then enter the Forêt Domaniale de Nore.

Beyond the Col de Salette you descend to the north on a broom-bristling road flanked by undulating green hills. At a junction turn right on the D920 for ST-PONS. Some 3km further on come to **Roc Suzadou** (📷🏠P), with a tremendous view over this bucolic countryside. An avenue of gorgeous chestnut trees welcomes you to the lovely hamlet of **Aymard**. Keep following ST-PONS, to reach the N112 at **Courniou** (63.5km). The **Grotte de la**

La Cité was first fortified by the Romans (1BC) because it lay on the road from the Atlantic to the Mediterranean. Visigoths, Franks, and successive counts carried on the work, until it was interrupted by the wars against the Cathars (see box page 63), when the town fell in 15 days. At that time there was only one set of walls (surrounding the Château Comtal, shown here), but later in the century Louis IX added an outer wall, beyond the moat. It was then considered impregnable, but history played a cruel trick. Roussillon was annexed, and Carcassonne lost its strategic importance to Perpignan, a town closer to the border. La Cité fell into decay; there was even talk of demolition. But 19th-century Romanticism saw a revival of interest in the Middle Ages; restoration began in 1844 and is on-going. Notice the slit-holes for archers in the walls and towers, and the wooden gallery, which allowed the defenders to hurl projectiles vertically downwards. Several towers have a projecting 'prow' on the outer side (not shown), which helped to deflect incoming projectiles and battering rams.

Devèze★ is signposted to the left; it is in fact almost opposite, on the road to the railway station. Turn right on the N112 and continue to **St-Pons-de-Thomières** (68.5km ♣M🛈), seat of the Regional Park. On approaching the splendid 12c cathedral, park in the small square on your right (Place Forail). The excellent tourist office, where Walk 16 begins, is just behind you.

From here head north on the plane tree-lined D907 for LA SALVETAT. (After passing the road to Brassac off to the left, keep an eye out after 0.8km for two stone gateposts and a signpost, CAMPING VERT, on your right: you can drop walkers off here for Short walk 16.) You climb into the Monts de l'Espinouse. Cross the Col du Cabaretou, coming down into fields with spring flowers, conifers and beech (🎄). Soon a hairpin-bend descent offers fine views (📷) down over picturesque La Salvetat, at the confluence of the Agout and Vèbre.

Do *not* cross the bridge to enter the village; bear left, then take the second right (LAC DE LA RAVIEGE). Pass a dairy on your left and then go left, again following LAC DE LA RAVIEGE. You come over a hill, and the lake stretches before you. Cross a bridge and go right (TOUR DU LAC), to skirt the northern side of the lovely **Lac de la Raviège**, a watersports centre. Shortly after this turn, there is a fine view to the right (📷) over La Salvetat in the valley, below the backdrop of the Espinouse.

When you meet the D52 turn sharp left for ANGLES, crossing the dam. Then continue for a further 1km, to follow the D52 into **Anglès**. Here keep straight ahead through two junctions, following BRASSAC. At the Col du Fauredon, go left on the D53 for BOUISSET and MAZAMET. **Bouisset** is a stark village, enlivened only by its bright green well of *eau potable* in the centre; in contrast, **Le Rialet** is a pretty red-roofed hamlet. Beyond here you climb into a 'cathedral' of beech and pines. Pass a small dam on the right at **Le Vintrou** and go right on the D54 immediately beyond it.

Come down towards Mazamet. Now you see the 'Black Mountain' from its most impressive angle: dark granite slopes, clad with firs, rise abruptly from the Thoré plain. Follow CENTRE VILLE, to enter the spreading industrial town of **Mazamet** (138.5km ♣M🛈) by ①. When you can, start following CARCASSONNE.* Watch for

---

*To park for Walk 17, watch for the pointed spire of Notre-Dame on the left (just over the railway). As soon as you pass it, turn right for TOUTES DIRECTIONS, CARCASSONNE. Cross a bridge, keep following TOUTES

the octagonal tower of St-Sauveur on your left: 400m beyond it, turn left on the D54 for PRADELLES, PIC DE NORE.

You enter the **Gorges de l'Arnette** and soon climb hard by the river, past a series of picturesque stone-built, red-roofed leather works and woollen mills; the river tumbles down over weirs beside you. Some 3km along this road turn off left to TREBY, PIC DE NORE. (This is where you should deposit walkers for Short walk 17.) Beyond the honey-coloured hamlet of **Les Yés** the mountain views open up. **Tréby** is a forestry house where Black Mountain troups regrouped in June 1944. Climb above beech and firs (Forêt de Nore) to a wind-buffeted moonscape, where a rocket-like TV transmitter beckons — the **Pic de Nore★** (1210m/3970ft; 156.5km 📷). The Espinouse and Lacune massifs rise in the north; in the south the Corbières and Pyrenees are visible.

Turn back from the viewpoint and, just past the relay station, go left on the D87 for CARCASSONNE. Ahead, dark conifers pierce the bright canopy of deciduous trees. **Pradelles-Cabardès** is a holiday village in the midst of woods and flower-drenched meadows. At the junction with the D112 go left. From the watershed of the **Col de la Prade**, you descend in zigzags back into the dry Mediterranean landscape of the **Gorges de la Clamoux.** A solitary patch of vineyards is glimpsed far below — at **Cabrespine** (173.5km 🗓), where a ruined château rises on the right. Attractive cultivation lines the gorge further downhill. Bear left at the next fork. A 12c tower on the main road at **Villeneuve-Minervois** (◼) mimics Carcassonne with its slate roof. Keep following CAR-CASSONNE, to stay on the D112 (ignore the D111 to Salsigne). Some 1.5km further south meet the D620 and retrace your outgoing route. In this flat landscape, the table-topped hill of Na Aurenque on your left, with its bib of vineyards, is a pretty picture on the approach to **Villegly**. Back in **Villalier** take the second left, just beyond the church. The D101, a quiet road arched with planes, takes you straight to **Trèbes**, where you cross the Canal du Midi (**P🚻**; Short walk 18-2).

From Trèbes follow CARCASSONNE, crossing the Aude. Keep in the right-hand lane (LA CITE) on the dual carriageway. Bear right on a slip road and loop back over the N113, to return to the **Porte Narbonnaise** (201km).

DIRECTIONS, then take the second left (Edouard Barbey). *Again* take the second left, into Place Gambetta. Now keep straight ahead in the one-way circuit to a large parking area at Champ de la Ville.

Tour 11: CORBIERES, LAND OF THE CATHARS

Carcassonne • Lagrasse • Château de Quéribus • (towards the Pyrenees) • Duilhac-sous-Peyrepertuse • Gorges de Galamus • Couiza • Limoux • Carcassonne

*195km/121mi; about 7h driving as a **one-day tour** or approximately 340km/211mi; 12-13h as a **two-day tour**; Michelin map 86 or 235*

En route: ⊞ at Gorges d'Alsou, (Vinça, Défilé de Pierre-Lys); P at the Grau de Maury, river Verdouble, (Pic de Baou, Ansignan); Walk 19

*There are quite a few narrow roads on this tour; the short stretches to the Châteaux of Termes and Peyrepertuse (both detours) and the road in the Gorges de Galamus are especially difficult if you meet on-coming traffic. The longest stretch without petrol is between Lagrasse and Rouffiac (72km). If you have time for a **two-day tour**, see page 67; you can head south from the Grau de Maury **towards the Pyrenees**, perhaps breaking your journey within sight of Canigou.*

This tour winds up into the Corbières, last great strong-hold of the Cathars. Bounded on the north by the Aude, this upland region rises between the Montagne Noire (Car tour 10) and the Pyrenees. Up until the conquest of Roussillon from Spain, the Corbières were of great strategic importance to France as a bulwark against the kingdom of Aragón. After the fall of the Cathars at Carcassonne, Louis IX fortified La Cité and five more sites in the Corbières — Puilaurens, Peyre-pertuse, Quéribus, Termes and Aguilar. These castles, recaptured Albigensian strongholds, became known as the 'five sons of Carcassonne'. With the annexation of

The gorgeous village of Termes, on the banks of the Orbieu. Its château fell to de Montfort in 1210 after a siege of four months and was later fortified by St-Louis. To visit the ruins (30min return on foot), cross the bridge before you come into the centre, and turn right up the narrow motorable track (0.5km each way). Note that this track is only wide enough for one car and there are no passing places.

Wherever you drive in this part of southwest France, you will see signposts proudly proclaiming that you are in the **land of the Cathars**. Catharism, a doctrine of 'purity', took hold in the Languedoc in the early 12th century, in great part as a reaction against the excesses of the church of Rome. Centred on Albi, its adherents (also called **Albigensians**) fanned out to the south and east, and soon boasted their own bishops and strongholds, including Carcassonne. They counted among their adherents wealthy merchants, artisans and professional people. At this time the Languedoc was in the hands of the Counts Raymond of Toulouse, humanists who tolerated this heretical sect. But the Cathars were a thorn in the side of Rome, and their success led to their eventual downfall and eradication. When his envoy was assassinated near St-Gilles (Tour 6) in 1208, Pope Innocent III determined to eradicate the heretics. A 'crusade' was mounted. First Béziers fell, then Carcassonne. Although the wars intensified from 1210, under Simon de Montfort's 'scorched earth' policy, only in 1229 was a truce imposed. Even then a few pockets of resistance remained. It took the Inquisition and the burning to death of 200 Cathars at Montségur in 1244 to eradicate the scourge of the 'pure ones'. The kings of France were only too happy to help Rome suppress the sect; they saw the great spoils to be gained. In 1271 Languedoc was officially annexed to France.

Roussillon in 1658 these fortresses lost their strategic importance and fell into ruin, as did Carcassonne.

Leave **Carcassonne** by ②, the N113. Just as you enter **Trèbes** turn right on the D3 for FONTIES D'AUDE, LAGRASSE. Some 5km along, a green basin of vineyards below a hill opens up ahead. A land of *garrigues* interspersed with hard-won vineyards, the Corbières yield a rich and fruity wine with a high alcohol content. The vines luxuriate on this calcareous soil; the Romans cultivated the grape in this region. Keep following LAGRASSE through **Monze** and **Pradelles-en-Val**. Beyond the hamlet of **Villemagne** you enter the heavily-wooded **Gorges d'Alsou** (⌂ with fireplaces). Then enjoy a fine view over Lagrasse on the right as you descend to the village.

On entering **Lagrasse★** (34km ⚓■ℹ) look right as you cross the bridge over the Orbieu, to see the 11c bridge and 8c abbey dating from the reign of Charlemagne. Park and wander the alleys of this gorgeous fortified village, not missing the covered 13c market or the highly-decorated 14c church. While catering for up-market tourism, Lagrasse remains unspoilt. Continue straight ahead through the village and, at the junction 3.5km outside it, turn right on the D23 for TALAIRAN, CHATEAU DE TERMES. *Almost immediately* go left (same signposting) and quickly follow that up with a right, the

D212 for ST-PIERRE, CHATEAU DE TERMES. Beyond **St-Pierre-des-Champs** you follow the sinuous Orbieu through a gorge. A lovely little R church stands on the right as you enter honey-hued **St-Martin-des-Puits**. The mountains become more prominent now and, on rounding a bend you pass below the beautiful ruins of the **Château de Durfort** (☐), rising above a meander of the river on the left. This château was abandoned without a fight on the arrival of de Montfort.

Just after circling Durfort, go left for TERMES on the D40 through the Gorges du Terminet, a chaos of rock and holly oaks. Round a bend to see the Château de Termes straight ahead. Admire the flower-filled setting of **Termes** (55.5km ☐; see photograph caption on page 62), then continue on the D40 south, along a crest between two wooded ravines. The road is only wide enough for one car, but there are passing places. Notice the creative topiary of the box hedges at the side of the road here … in the 'middle of nowhere'. At the **Col de Bedos** turn left on the D613 for FELINES; over to the right there is a gentle valley backed by mountains. In spring this stretch is awash with golden broom and white-flowering false acacias. Just after entering the confines of **Félines**, turn sharp right on the D39 for TUCHAN. Then go right again on the D139 for DAVEJEAN and MAISONS. In the centre of **Davejean** turn left on the D10 for MAISONS.

Climb above the red roofs of Davejean on a narrow road. Under 2km further on, at the Col du Prat, go left on the D410. At the end of **Maisons** continue south on the D123 for PADERN. The D410 turns off right for Mont-gaillard. Ignore this turn; go sharp left on the D123 for PADERN. You head straight for the Montagne de Tauch. Considering the foothills that have gone before, we're in impressive mountains now. Via the gorges of the river Torgan come to **Padern** (84km ☐), where another ruined castle on the left dominates the village. After crossing a bridge over the Verdouble, you reach a junction with the D14. (*Here you could turn left for a 21km return detour through the Fitou vineyards to Tuchan and one of the 'five sons' — the 13c Château d'Aguilar; ☐.*)

The main tour turns right here for CUCUGNAN, following the D14 southwest along the valley of the Ver-double. Having passed below **Cucugnan**, go left on the D14 for PEYREPERTUSE, QUERIBUS; then, *just 100m further on,* turn sharp left uphill on the D123 for MAURY. You climb above the honey and red cluster of Cucugnan.

The Château of Puilaurens (Towards the Pyrenees, page 70)

Straight ahead the château of Quéribus rises on a rocky spike. Two kilometres uphill, at the **Grau de Maury★** (🔄*P*), turn left and climb to the parking area for the **Château de Quéribus★** (93km 🕐). From here the whole plain of Roussillon is at your feet, with Canigou rising in the Pyrenees as a centrepiece. Nearby, in the north-west, the silhouette of Peyrepertuse blends so well into a limestone ridge that it is hardly perceptible. While the holocaust at Montségur in 1244 is acknowledged as the turning point in the war against the Cathars, the last battle was fought here at Quéribus in 1255.

On the descent from the castle there is a fine view of the Verdouble Valley. At the Grau de Maury (*P* straight ahead, under the trees), turn right, back towards Cucugnan. *Or, if you are taking an extra day to see the Pyrenees, turn left and refer to the notes on page 67.* At the junction with the D14 turn left and again follow the Verdouble Valley — the most intensively-cultivated stretch on the main tour. Vineyards stretch away on both sides of the road, fringed by wooded slopes below white limestone crags. At the entrance to **Duilhac-sous-Peyrepertuse** (101km)* keep straight ahead for ROUFFIAC on the D14. Just after passing the *boulangerie* in the

*To visit the **Château de Peyrepertuse★** (🕐🔄), take the *very narrow, vertiginous* road at the entrance to Duilhac *(a detour of 7km return; plus 1h return on foot)*. From Rouffiac you will have a much better view of Peyrepertuse — the largest of the 'sons of Carcassonne'. With ramparts over 300m/1000ft long, it covered an area equal in size to the Cité of Carcassonne! This Cathar stronghold was so inaccessible that even de Montfort dare not lay siege to it. Peyrepertuse was the base for a final attempt to retake Carcassonne (1240); when this failed the castle fell to the royal army without a battle.

The brilliant white limestone flanks of the Pic de Bugarach rise up from a grassy plain like a crumpled fedora; it is an almost huggable mountain, and the urge to climb it is irresistible.

lower part of Duilhac, park near the hotel if you are doing Walk 19, or use the map on page 128 to picnic beside the Verdouble (*P*). If you need petrol, turn off right into the centre of tiny Rouffiac-des-Corbières (⛽), a delightful flower-bound hamlet. Otherwise continue straight ahead (with fine views up left to Peyrepertuse). Notice the tangerine-coloured stone of the simple church at **Soulatge**.

Little parcelled gardens hide behind the stone walls at **Cubières-sur-Cinoble** (115km). In the centre turn left on the D10 for ST-PAUL-DE-FENOUILLET, to climb a very narrow road through the **Gorges de Galamus★**. Although the gorge is not very long, its high vertical white rock walls make this one of the most impressive gorges in the eastern Pyrenees. After 4km, just before a tunnel, park in a large layby. Take the path and long flight of steps down to the hermitage St-Antoine-de-Galamus (✝✖🗟), to admire the fine view over the most impressive part of the gorge. (Just beyond the tunnel there is another parking area with a view to the hermitage and a wine-tasting kiosk, but it's a longer walk to the chapel.)

From here return to Cubières and turn left on the D14, to follow the valley of the Agly, a beautiful swathe of green and gold cultivation. Soon you pass to the right of the **Pic de Bugarach★** (1230m/4035ft; photograph above), the highest mountain in the Corbières. Pass to the left of **Bugarach** village, then follow the wooded gorge of the Blanque. The river, hard on our right, enlivens the approach to **Rennes-les-Bains**. Just 3km beyond Rennes turn left on the D613 for COUIZA. Severely pollarded plane trees, with slender branches sticking upright like matchsticks, introduce **Couiza** (151km ⛪)

with a well-preserved château and bridge (both 16c). At the traffic lights go straight over for ALET and LIMOUX, following a dual carriageway with an avenue of planes.

The road bypasses the centre of **Alet-les-Bains** (where there is a ruined 11CR cathedral) and comes into **Limoux** via more eccentrically-pollarded planes (166km ✚ⓘ). Limoux is best known for its carnival and sparkling wine (*blanquette*). Keep following CARCASSONNE. As soon as you go through the first roundabout, immediately fork right for ST-HILAIRE (poor signposting). Cross the Aude again and look right to see the old 15c bridge and spire of the 13/16CG church. Unfortunately there is nowhere to pull up to enjoy this view. Turn left for PIEUSSE and ST-HILAIRE; just over 1km further on you pass the G pilgrimage chapel of Notre-Dame de Marceille on the left. Bypass Pieusse, another outpost of the Cathars.

Descend to **St-Hilaire** (✝) in a cradle of vineyards, passing to the right of the R/G church and 14c cloister. It was the Benedictine monks of St-Hilaire who reputedly discovered the secret of *blanquette*. Go straight ahead and cross the Lauquet. After 3km, on coming to a fork, go right (still on the D104). Bypass the centre of **Verzeille** and come into **Leuc**. Cross the river and head left for COUFFOULENS but, at a Y-fork under 2km further on, bear right for CAVANAC. You come over a hill and look down on the plain of Carcassonne. Keep following CARCASSONNE CENTRE. When you come to a stop sign at a T-junction, turn left on the D142. Just after passing under the motorway turn right for CAMPING DE LA CITE. Soon you have a brilliant view of **La Cité**, especially attractive at twilight. After passing the Camping de la Cité on the left, *watch carefully* for a small wine-red sign on the right, HOTEL MERCURE LA VICOMTE. Turn right here; the road leads to the Porte Narbonnaise (195km).

Towards the Pyrenees

From the Grau de Maury (0km) continue south to **Maury** (ⓘ), with its huge wine cooperatives. Follow ESTAGEL, PERPIGNAN, to leave Maury on the D117. In the centre of **Estagel** turn right on the D612 for MONTNER. Pass the turn-off for this hamlet and continue ahead for MILLAS. At the **Col de la Bataille** turn left uphill (the road is not built up at the edge, but is amply wide). After 4km park on the right, at the hermitage of **Forca Réal★** (✝), from where there is a superb view over the plain and the coast. Inland, Quéribus rises like a needle from the crests and, further west, the Pic de Bugarach can be recognised by its two distinct peaks. As you descend from the hermitage, there is a superb view over the Pyrenees villages south of the N116, with Canigou behind them. Back at the col, turn left. After 5km turn right and cross the Têt, to enter **Millas** (36.5km). In the centre of the village you meet the very busy N116. When you get a break in the traffic, turn left for PERPIGNAN but, after only 0.6km (just after crossing the Boulès) turn right on the D612 for THUIR. For a while you follow a beautiful avenue of planes. After crossing the D16 signposted right for Corbère, take the *next* right, the D58 for CAMELAS. In early summer you can reach out and touch the peaches along this road. After 2km come to the D615 and turn left, then go right immediately for CASTELNOU. A narrow road (☎) takes you to **Castelnou★**, straddling a knoll in a green basin. This wonderfully picturesque medieval Catalan village is a beehive of molasses-coloured stone and salmon roofs, surrounded by a bib of vineyards. Follow CAIXAS to leave Castelnou on the D48. The summit of Canigou is straight ahead; in the middle distance the chapel of St-Martin rises across the valley, on a mountain to your right. Behind it is the omnipresent Quéribus. When you meet the D2, turn sharp right for ST-MICHEL-DE-LLOTES. The isolated chapel of Fontcouverte (✝) stands off to the right here in a desolate landscape.

Drop down in hairpin bends to **St-Michel-de-Llotes** and pass below its R church on the right. On meeting the D16, bear left for BOULETERNERE. Immediately come to a roundabout; take 2nd exit, D16 for BOULETERNERE, passing orchards of peach, cherry and plum trees. At **Bouleternère** an old R church rises at top of the village. In the centre turn right and right again 200m further on, to keep on the D16 for VINÇA and PRADES. Come to the N116 and turn left. After 4km pass the parking area for the Barrage de Vinça (⊼), with a R chapel. Just under 2km further on bypass Vinça, where there is a lovely R chapel. Cross the Lentilla and enter **Marquixanes**, once again with a R church tower on the left. Now, if you have *Landscapes of the Pyrenees* and plan to climb Canigou, take a kilometre reading as you pass the sign denoting the end of Marquixanes: 3km past here

Picnic beside a deserted farmstead, looking over towards Canigou

you pass the D24 left to LOS MASOS. You can take this road to join the Villerach road for the ascent of Canigou (or take the exit signposted to VILLERACH off the roundabout 2km further on). Come into **Prades** (84.5km 🅸). At the roundabout follow CENTRE VILLE. Not long after passing to the left of the R church (still on the D116), turn left on the D27 for CODALET, TAURINYA.

This road takes you past the **Abbaye St-Michel-de-Cuxa★** (✝), where for many years Pablo Casals took charge of the Prades music festival. Canigou rises behind the abbey, its summit snow-capped for much of the year. One of most important religious buildings in the South of France, the 10c abbey was founded for the Benedictines. During the Revolution, parts of the building (at that time abandoned) were sold; later a good number of the original columns found their way to the banks of the Hudson River in New York (as did the cloisters of St-Guilhem-le-Désert, visited in Car tour 8). Today the abbey is under the care of Catalonian monks from Montserrat; set in peach tree orchards, it almost has the appearance of a *domaine*. Climb past the attractive 11CR church in **Taurinya** to the Col de Millères. (From here another road goes towards Canigou, but it is only suitable for the excursion jeeps that frequent it; *route difficile* on the Michelin map.) Pass the ruined R Tour de Cours on the right and, just before the centre of **Fillols** (where there is another attractive R church tower), fork right for CORNEILLA. Soon the village is visible in the valley, below a high red escarpment. Curl down into **Corneilla-de-Conflent** (✝) and squeeze past the fine 11/12CR church with its square tower on your right and a round tower on your left. From there go on to the beautiful medieval village of **Ville-franche-de-Conflent★** (114km ✝🔳🅸). Visit the 12c church of St-Jacques and the ramparts. First fortified by Spain to confront the 'five sons of Carcassonne', some of the original 11c walls remain, but the ramparts are chiefly the work of Vauban (17c).

At a fork head left to keep on the N116 to PRADES; the Conflent is on your left. This raceway goes through **Ria**. Ignore signs for Prades now; keep on the ring road, following PERPIGNAN and bearing left at a fork. Then, at a roundabout, ignore 'Perpignan'; follow CATLAR, the second exit. You turn sharp left back on yourself and then head right on the D619 for CATLAR and MOLITG. Pass Mas Riquer on the right and go through **Catlar**. Cross the Castellane and, 1km further on, turn sharp right on the D619 for SOURNIA. There are magnificent views to Canigou as you climb this narrow road through *garrigues* — the mountain is visible from top to bottom, rising up from the plain. Some 10km along come to a deserted house on the right, where you can picnic in the setting shown opposite (📷*P*), the *only shade* in these sun-drenched *garrigues*. Some 2km past here, at the **Pic de Baou/Col de Roque Jalère** (📷), there is just room to pull over on the right and look north over the huge basin of the Fenouillèdes, with the Corbières range and the Château de Peyrepertuse in the distance. The wedge of the Pic de Bugarach rises to the west of Sournia, which is seen below. Pass the oddly-shaped Roc Cornut on the left and keep ahead for SOURNIA (where a road goes right to Campoussy).

A quarry rises behind unremarkable **Sournia** (128km 🚐). At the T-junction turn right on the D619 for ST-PAUL. Almost immediately come to a fork and go right for PEZILLA (D619). After 4km ignore the wide D2 to Trevillach; go left downhill for PEZILLA on a narrower road. Stone walled terraces enhance the approach to **Pézilla-de-Conflent**, where a R tower rises on the left above the red roof-tops. At a junction 3km outside Pézilla, keep ahead on the D619 for ANSIGNAN. Just 0.7km beyond the signpost denoting the entrance to **Ansignan** turn right on the D9 for TRILLA. A lovely view over vineyards opens up on the left; they hide a treasure. Under 1km further on, turn sharp left downhill on a very narrow country lane (small signpost, AQUEDUC). Cross a stream and then turn left again; soon you see the aqueduct★ (*P*) shown on page 6, spanning the Agly. Return to Ansignan the same way, looking back over the setting (several 📷).

Back at Ansignan, turn right for ST-PAUL. The high limestone crags of the most southerly Corbières rise just in front of you as you follow the wooded Agly gorge. Cross a bridge in a very pretty setting, with the ruins of an old Roman bridge ahead. In **St-Paul-de-Fenouillet** (153km), you have a choice; distances for both routes are approximately the same. Either go north through the GORGES DE GALAMUS★ and pick up the main tour in Cubières (the 115km-point), or go via Quillan and pick up the main tour at Couiza (151km-point).

To go via Quillan, at St-Paul follow AUTRES DIRECTIONS by going right at a Y-fork. At the light turn left on the D117 for FOIX and cross the Agly. Pass through the outskirts of **Caudiès-de-Fenouillet** and, 6km further on (just after crossing the Boulzane), turn left on the D22 for the Château de Puilaurens (*not signposted and easily missed*). Its crenellated silhouette soon towers above you in a dramatic setting (photograph page 65), with the river on the left. In **Puilaurens** turn right on a good road to the castle (🅿; 45min return on foot). This Cathar stronghold became the 'son of Carcassonne' closest to Aragón.

Return to the D117 and turn left for QUILLAN, beside the Aude (🍴). Bypass Axat, then cross the Aude and follow the narrow **Défilé de Pierre-Lys**, where the river threads through limestone cliffs (🍴). This is a main road used by lorries but, when you can, pull over to look at the rushing river and take in some negative ions. The lovely old part of **Belvianes** is seen off to the right, then the Aude spills over a weir. The wide moss-green river and the plane-shaded road enhance the approach to **Quillan** (194km ℹ). A thriving market and manufacturing town, Quillan is also a good walking base. (*From here Cathar devotees can take a detour west on the D117 to the imposing ruins of the Château de Puivert; 32km return.*) Keep straight ahead through Quillan, following LIMOUX and still skirting the Aude to rejoin the main tour at Couiza.

❁ Walking

Those who go to France purely for a walking holiday are likely to be tackling the long linear GR routes. *This book has been written for motorists who want to tour the most beautiful roads and enjoy some glorious walks en route.* Very few of the walks are strenuous, and we don't include hikes to summits that are easily reached by car (like Ventoux). The walks have been chosen to highlight the great variety of landscapes in the South of France and to focus on our favourite beauty spots.

Although the walks are scattered between Aix and the Pyrenees, you should find several within easy reach (no more than an hour away by car or public transport) no matter where you are based. If you are staying in one area for a couple of weeks, visit the nearest *syndicat d'initiative* (tourist office) to get information about local walks and up-to-date **bus and train timetables** (many of our walks are accessible by public transport; see 'How to get there' at the top of the relevant page).

Weather

All the walks in this book may be done the year round, but from mid-June to mid-September it will be far too hot to enjoy any but the easiest rambles (almost all involve *some* climbing, and there is usually no water source en route). Spring and autumn are the best seasons for walking; not only are the temperatures moderate, but there is an extravaganza of wild flowers and seasonal foliage. On the other hand, you will have to put up with a few days of torrential rain. In winter the landscape is more monotone, but the weather is usually dry, clear and cool. The notorious *mistral* blows for about a third of the year (usually in winter and spring and usually for a *minimum* of three days).

The banks of the Hérault near the Pont du Diable make a lovely picnic setting during Car tour 8.

71

Le 'Petit Train' in the Gorges d'Héric is an amusing way to get to the start of Short walk 14-1 or 14-2. This is just a 'toddler' but, when you are walking in Alpes-Maritimes or Alpes de Haute-Provence, you can take the delightful 'Train des Pignes', to get to several walks (see South of France: The Alps to Aix).

Often it is difficult to stand upright, and no walks should be attempted in areas exposed to this northerly wind.

What to take

No special equipment is needed for any of the walks, but proper **walking boots** are preferable to any other footwear. Most walks in the South of France cross very stony terrain at some stage, and good ankle support is essential. In the wet weather you will also be glad of the waterproofing. A **sunhat** and high-protection **suncream** are equally important; there is a real risk of sunstroke on some walks. Each member of the party should carry a small rucksack, so that the chore of lugging the essentials is shared. *All year round* it is advisable to carry a first-aid kit, whistle, torch, spare socks and bootlaces, and some warm clothing (the mistral can blow up suddenly, with temperatures dropping up to 10°C/20°F!). A long-sleeved shirt and long trousers should be worn or carried, both for sun protection and for making your way through the prickly plants of the *maquis*. Depending on the season, you may also need an anorak, lightweight rainwear, woollies and gloves. Optional items include swimwear, a Swiss Army knife, plastic cups and flasks, insect repellent. Mineral water is sold almost everywhere in plastic half-litre bottles; *it is imperative that each walker carries at least a half-litre of water — a full litre in hot weather.*

Nuisances

We have never been bothered by dogs but, for peace of mind, you might like to invest in an ultrasonic **dog** deterrent: contact Dazer UK, 51 Alfriston Road, London SW11 6NR. Any snakes you may spot slithering out of your way will probably be harmless, but **vipers** (recognisable by the distinct triangular shape of the head) *do* exist (another good reason always to wear boots and long trousers). Take care if you move a log or stone, and *always* keep a look-out near dry-stone walls. Outside winter you may be plagued by an encyclopaedic array of **biting insects** — just when you are panting up a mountain or tucking into lunch. You may also encounter **beehives** along some of the routes; bees are not a problem if you keep your distance.

Waymarking, grading, safety

You will encounter **waymarking** on almost all the walks, but this is not necessarily helpful. Many routes have been waymarked over the years with different colours and symbols. Only the GR (Grande Randonnée) waymarking is meticulously maintained. Local councils change PR (Petite Randonnée) routes from year to year, often *without* removing old waymarks.* Moreover, **our walks do not always follow the waymarked routes**. Where waymarks are important, we refer to them in the text; otherwise *ignore them!* Do, however, note these waymarking features, common to both PR and GR routes:

— A *flash* (stripe of paint) or *dot* (stipple of paint) indicates 'Route continues this way'. (The GR uses *two separate* flashes, red and white, and this must *never* be confused with a red flash on a white paint background, which is forestry marking, *not* route marking.)
— An arrow with the flashes means 'Change of direction'.
— An X means 'Wrong way'.

The walks have been **graded** for the deskbound person who nevertheless keeps reasonably fit. Our timings average 4km per hour on the flat, plus 20 minutes for every 100m/300ft of ascent. None of the walks ascends more than about 600m/2000ft. *Do* check your timings against ours on a short walk before tackling one of the longer hikes. Remember that these are *neat walking times;* increase the overall time by at least one-third, to allow for lunch breaks and nature-watching.

Safety depends in great part on knowing what to expect* and being properly equipped. On *most* of our routes you will encounter other walkers — an advantage if you get into difficulty. Nevertheless, we advise

*For this reason *never* follow local footpath waymarks without the corresponding *up-to-date* route description or sketch map from the tourist office. You could find yourself on a dangerous path that has not been maintained for years. If you decide to do a walk not described in this book, *check the distance and the climb, then work out how long it will take* **you**. Some of the walks recommended by tourist offices are timed for very young, fit walkers. Beware, too, of any walks described as *sportif:* they are always potentially hazardous.

Farm in the Alpilles, near Les Baux

you **never** to walk alone, and **always** to tell someone where you are going and when you plan to return.

Maps

The **maps** in this book, adapted from the latest IGN 1:25,000 maps (Série Bleue) should see you through almost a month's walking. Most have been reproduced to a scale of 1:30,000 (about 2" to the mile; the scales are shown on all maps). If you buy any IGN maps to find new walks, note that the latest maps (TOP 25 Series) show many local and long-distance walks. But because these waymarked routes change from time to time (even a GR may be diverted), some routes will be out of date. We alert you to these map errors where they affect our walks. Older IGN maps show *only* GR routes *or none at all.* It is very difficult to plan a short or circular walk using these maps, because they do not indicate permissive routes: 'on the ground' you may come up against barbed wire or a new housing estate. If new IGN maps are not available, seek out up-to-date walk suggestions from the local tourist office.

While roads, tracks, railway lines, etc are easily identified on the IGN maps, below is a key to the most important symbols on our walking maps.

····· footpath	——— ski trail	cemetery
=== cart track	++++ kayak descent	P 🚗 car parking
=== waymarked	→ main walk	🚌 bus station/stop
== routes	⇨ alternative route	🚂 railway station
····· difficult route	♀ † church. cross	⭐ 👁 best views
woodland	● ▫ spring, water tank	⚡ pylon
boundary	⌐ ◣ dolmen. menhir	❶ *gendarmerie*

74

Walk 1: ROUSSILLON

Distance: 4km/2.5mi; 1h   **See also cover photograph**

Grade: easy, but agility is required to descend a few short but steep paths in the ochre quarries (some railings or ropes are in place).

Equipment: stout lace-up walking shoes, sunhat, water, optional picnic

How to get there: 🚌 (Car tour 1)

Short walk: Roussillon's ochre quarries (allow 30min-1h; grade as above). From the tourist office turn right and then left uphill past the cemetery, following the signposted SENTIER DES OCRES.

If red is your favourite colour, this walk is an eyeful of delight. In spring the rose-tipped leaves of the cherry trees flutter above a carpet of scarlet poppies; in autumn rusty-red leaves mask laden vines. And above these gently-farmed fields rises magnificently-sited Roussillon. The houses, painted in a spectrum of reds, sprout from rusty-red cliffs. Do this walk in the early morning, for the best light ... and do it in the direction suggested, to save the best — the fantastic 'sculptures' of the old ochre quarries — for last!

Start out at the tourist office and head north downhill along the Route de la Fontaine towards MURS. Ignore the turnings left (D169 to Gordes) and right (D227 to Murs and St-Saturnin); go straight ahead on the C7 for CLAVAILLAN. Some 200m/yds further on, there is a Y-fork on the right: go right here, on the Chemin de St-Michel (orange arrow on a telephone pole). Straight away come to another Y-fork and go left on a grassy track, ignoring a track up to the right. A vineyard is on your left. There are fine views now of vineyards stretching away to the northeast, as you continue under beech and oak.

Cross the St-Saturnin road (D227; **15min**) and follow it a few paces to the left uphill, then go right on a track through vineyards (where a track goes left to Château Blanc). The track heads up left towards the cherry tree-covered hill of Pied de Bœuf and then swings right below the hill, to head towards an ocre and white cliff on the hill of Pierroux. Look back towards Roussillon from here, brilliant in the morning sun.

At **30min** reach the D199 and turn right. Ten minutes along, just past a transformer, turn right into Le Hameau des Ocres. Keep ahead past some letter-boxes on your right and come to a Y-fork. Bear right here, keeping more letter-boxes on your right. At the next fork go right again; this time keep the letter-boxes to your left. Now you leave the tarmac and go ahead on an earthen path. At the next fork go left.

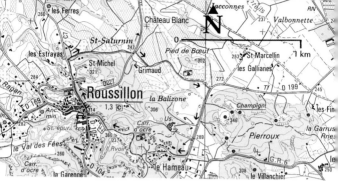

All of a sudden you've entered the old ochre quarries, a fantastic landscape of grotesquely-eroded forms. The Mediterranean pines and acacias come into their own now, their subtle shades of green a perfect foil for the vibrant ochre hues — ranging from white to deep gold, sienna, copper, burgundy and deepest purple. From now on follow the signposted nature trail which will take you to all the whimsically-named sculptures in this 'museum' — the 'circle of needles', the 'fairies' chimneys', the 'giants' causeway'. They are the result of rainwater erosion, and their shapes are changing with the centuries.

Having slipped and slithered your way through the quarries, come upon a paved walkway and descend past the cemetery on your left to the village centre where you started out (**1h**). Before leaving Roussillon, be sure to walk up past the church, to the *table d'orientation*.

A fluted, razor-sharp edge in the ochre quarries. Fragrant pines make this a delightful, shady picnic setting. These mineral deposits are 90 per cent sand and, after removing the impurities, only two percent of what is mined results in the ochre pigment. Roussillon's quarries opened in 1780, but competition from artificial colourants finally resulted in their closure 100 years later.

Walk 2: GORDES • SENANQUE • ABBAYE DE SENANQUE • GORDES

Distance: 9.5km/6mi; 3h10min

Grade: easy-moderate, with ascents totalling 300m/1000ft. The paths and tracks are fairly stony, and there is little shade en route.

Equipment: stout lace-up walking shoes (walking boots preferable), sunhat, picnic, water

How to get there: 🚗 (Car tour 2) or 🚌 to Gordes

Shorter walk: Gordes — Abbaye de Sénanque — Gordes (5.5km/ 3.4mi; 2h20min; access/equipment/grade as above, with ascents totalling about 250m/820ft). Follow the GR6 to the Abbaye de Sénanque and return the same way. Start out in the main square. Facing the Café Provençal (with the château behind you), take the road to the left, walking past the Hotel Bastide on the left. Ignore the road up right to the *gendarmerie;* cross over to the *immobilier* (estate agent), and turn left on the pavement in front of it. Watch for a fountain with non-potable water on your right, and turn sharp right uphill on a lane just past it. Beyond a wooden gate on your right, you pick up a red and white GR waymark (5min from the Café Provençal). On meeting the D177 go right but, after 200m, go left at a Y-fork (GR waymark) When you next meet the D177, bear left and follow it to a signpost, COTES DE SENANQUE (fine viewpoint). Now continue ahead to another sign, GARAGE 180M, on your right. On your left a sign indicating a curve in the road ahead bears GR flashes: the path down left to the abbey is just behind the sign.

NB: The abbey (paid admission) is closed from 12.00-15.00.

T he magnificent Abbaye de Sénanque, founded by Cistercian monks in the 12th century, is the focal point for this walk. A wonderful feeling of tranquillity pervades these buildings.

Start out in the main square at Gordes. Facing the Café Provençal (with the château behind you), ignore the road to Murs at the right of the café, take the *next* road to the right, descending past the post office on your right. At a Y-fork, bear right, keeping the dry-stone walls of the cemetery to your left. If you look carefully, you will spot blue flashes on the wall; these waymarks are followed for the first part of the walk. Beyond the cemetery gate (**5min**), the lane eventually loses its tarred surface. When you come onto tarmac again, by a house, keep straight ahead, still following the blue waymarks. Just past here, at a Y-fork, go left, with magnificent dry-stone walls* on either side. Then meet the D15 and go straight ahead.

*There is an association in Vaucluse working for the preservation and restoration of dry-stone structures. One of their projects is especially fascinating: they are repairing the 12km-long 'Mur de la Peste', built in the 1720s between Monieux and Cabrières (Car tour 4) to halt the spread of the plague which was racing north from Marseille. At the height of the epidemic, 1000 soldiers manned this dry-stone wall.

Rows of lavender lead the eye to the Abbaye de Sénanque.

Some **25min** into the walk turn left uphill at a sign-post for FONTANILLE. At the next fork, by the campsite, go left. You quickly come to some letter-boxes, where you turn right on a tarmac lane (blue flashes). The tarmac runs out and you come to a fork, where a track goes left. Take the stony path to the right — just a short-cut which rejoins the track. When the track turns off to the left, take the path straight ahead, heading due north, with fields to your right. The narrow path runs through *garrigues*, where stunted oaks provide some shade. Clumps of tiny blue grass lilies (*Aphyllanthes monspeliensis*) dot the path; they flower in May and June.

At **1h05min**, at the end of the fields, we come to a T-junction (spot height 517). There's a huge pine tree here, offering good shade for picnicking. Turn right but, after 150m/yds, go left down a footpath (blue flashes *and red dots*). This wide stony path descends into the Vallon de Ferrière — a basin of lavender cultivation. Cross the valley and then climb gently to the left of the lavender, ignoring the entrance to the farm on your right. The Sénancole Valley opens up on the left now. At a fork, where a path goes straight ahead, keep left on a stony track and follow it southwest along the crest. Soon you have glimpses of the abbey, and you can see the Lubéron in the distance, rising from the plain.

In **1h30min**, meet a crossing track near the hamlet of Sénanque. Turn right downhill; the track curves left and into an open wood, another pleasant, shady picnic spot. Five minutes later you reach a crossroads with several tracks *and no waymarking*. Keep straight ahead here on the level, motorable track. It passes to the right of a pecan grove and a large building, and takes you out to the D177 in five minutes. Cross the road and climb a path opposite (faded blue flash on a rock on the right after 20 paces). In three minutes you meet a crossing path bearing red and white GR flashes: turn down left and continue to the Abbaye de Sénanque (**2h05min**).

At the abbey walk to the left of the church, towards a cross. Climb to the left of the cross, and you will pick up the GR flashes quickly, curving uphill in *laçets* to the D177 (**2h30min**). Bear right on the road and follow it to a sign, COTES DE SENANQUE. Just beyond here, turn right downhill on a stony trail (GR flashes), from where you can see Gordes ahead. When you next meet the D177, follow it for 200m, then fork left with the GR down a lane. Meet the main road again, in Gordes: turn left, then curve right, into the centre (**3h10min**).

Walk 3: CIRCUIT AROUND BUOUX

Distance: 10km/6.2mi; 2h35min   See also photograph page 131

Grade: fairly easy, with ascents totalling under 200m/650ft. Good paths and tracks, but most of the ascents are in full sun.

Equipment: stout lace-up walking shoes (walking boots preferable), sunhat, picnic, water (there is also a water tap in Buoux).

How to get there: ⛟ to Séguin. Take the D113 east towards Buoux and turn off after 1.5km for LES SEGUINS; park just over 1km along, past the turn-off right to FORT DE BUOUX (Car tour 2).

Short walk: Séguin — Deyme — Séguin (5.5km/3.4mi; 1h25min; easy, with an initial ascent of 100m; equipment/access as above). Follow the main walk for 1h, then turn left on the road (D113). In just over 1km, where the road makes a tight bend to the right, go left for LES SEGUINS; your car is just past the turn-off right to the Fort de Buoux.

As you approach Séguin, a beautiful limestone edge suddenly appears on your left, on the far side of the Aigue-Brun Valley. This walk takes you along the top of the edge and then to a sunny plateau, before descending back into the valley beneath the slender tower of St-Symphorien and the ruins of the Fort de Buoux.

Start out by continuing east along the road. Where the road turns left to the inn at Séguin, head right on a path. Follow the blue cross waymarks (+), going downhill to the left when you come to a fork. At a second fork a minute later, again go left downhill. Now you have joined the GR9 and you cross the river (Aigue-Brun; **10min**) and then a narrow watercourse.

Soon you're on a beautiful old stone-laid trail that climbs in deep zigzags (*laçets*); make sure, just a few minutes up, that you turn sharp left into the first of these *laçets,* where another path goes straight ahead. At first the climbing edge towers above you on the left. After an easy climb of about 15 minutes you must head up left over bare rock: you'll see two vertical GR flashes

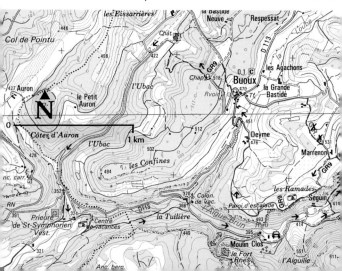

The extensive ruins of the Fort de Buoux, an oppidum inhabited from the Bronze Age until the reign of Louis XIV

and the word BUOUX painted in blue on a rock on your left. At the top of this small rise, where SEGUIN is painted in blue and an arrow points back the way you came, turn left. Now a lovely earthen path takes you along the top of the climbing edge (**30min**) through holm and holly oaks. A farm (Marrenon) is hidden from view above on the right; soon you are skirting its stone walls.

Enjoy fine views down left over the Aigue-Brun Valley and, after about 15 minutes, towards the ruined Fort de Buoux almost opposite. After about **45min** a shed on the right bears GR waymarks, and the GR turns right here (it is incorrectly shown on the IGN map). Continue *straight ahead* along the cliff-edge, following blue *dot* waymarks. Lavender fields sweep away to your right, on the other side of a wall. Soon the path swings north, and the houses of Buoux come into view on the slopes ahead. A gentle descent follows, through the hamlet of Deyme, where tarmac comes underfoot.

We soon join the D113 (**1h**). *The Short walk leaves us here and heads left downhill along this road.* Take the dirt track straight ahead, passing to the right of the popular Auberge de la Loube and cutting a bend off the road. When you reach the road again, turn right and pass to the left of a *gîte d'étape*. By **1h05min** you're in Buoux, where there is a tap on the right with welcome drinking water. Turn up left on a road just past the tap and just before a telephone kiosk; you rejoin the GR9 here (flashes on the road). Keep on tarmac, curling round to the left, to pass above a farm and then Buoux

81

church. Then follow the road in a hairpin bend to the right, passing a shrine on the left. At under **1h15min** come to a chapel, where the GR goes right on a track. Head left here through broom, to skirt the chapel on a footpath (notice the pale blue flash on a tree).

A stony path takes you down into the Ubac Valley and to the Renaissance Château de Buoux (**1h30min**). At the château turn left on the stony access track and follow it round to left, to a surfaced road. Head straight downhill on this pretty road; tiny fields on the right, shaded by oaks, make pleasant picnic spots. You meet the D113 on a hairpin bend (**1h50min**): turn right, again following the pale blue flashes. In under two minutes (after about 100m/yds), turn left down a track sign-posted FONTBRUME. Three minutes or so downhill come to a junction and turn left on a track marked with the same dark blue cross waymark that you followed at the start of the walk. Step over a chain barrier barring the track to vehicles; then, just in front of the gates of the Colonie de Vacances owned by the city of Marseille, turn right downhill on a track. After you pass to the right of some buildings, the track turns down to the right, and you cross a stream on a concrete footbridge, where you should see more pale blue flashes (**2h**).

Soon you can look back across the valley to the tower of St-Symphorien, rising above a fringe of oak leaves (photograph page 131). The path makes a U-turn and, beyond another of the holiday camp's 'private' signs, starts to climb. *Now keep watch* for your ongoing footpath, which comes in from behind and to the left *(very easily missed).* It is waymarked with pale blue flashes and dark blue crosses. On coming to a Y-fork a minute along this path, keep left on the main path hedged in by greenery. This shady footpath brings you back down to the Aigue-Brun. You pass a grassy area on the left with a lone picnic table and soon the path meets the road (**2h25min**), by another signpost for the Colonie de Vacances which bears the two sets of blue waymarks.

Head right along the road. If you're here on a weekend, you will be treated to the breath-taking spectacle of climbers swarming over the edge like flies on a honey-pot. If you haven't already visited the Fort de Buoux, do so now (allow about 1h). Or make for aptly named 'Needle Rock' (l'Aiguille); it rises just beyond your parking place, which is reached after **2h35min**.

Walk 4: FORÊT DES CEDRES

Distance: 7.5km/4.7mi; 2h25min

Grade: easy, with an initial descent and re-ascent of 100m/330ft; the rest of the walk is on almost level terrain; good surfaces underfoot.

Equipment: stout lace-up walking shoes (walking boots preferable), sunhat, picnic, water

How to get there: 🚌 to the Forêt des Cèdres, signposted off the D36 (1.5km south of Bonnieux). Paid parking after some 5km, at the barriers preventing access to the Route des Crêtes (Car tours 2, 4).

Short walks: equipment and access as above

1   Sentier Botanique (3km/2mi; 1h08min; grade as above). Follow the main walk for 1h05min, then return along the road to your car.

2   Roque des Bancs (5km/3mi; 1h25min; easy level walking). Follow the Route des Crêtes for 15 minutes, until you come to a water tank on your left. Now pick up the main walk at the 1h15min-point.

3   Viewpoint (2.2km/1.4mi; 30min; very easy). Follow the Route des Crêtes for 300m, then turn left on a wide path between two cairns, to reach a fine viewpoint by signpost N° 8. Return the same way.

Cedars from the Atlas Mountains of northern Africa were introduced on the heights of the Petit Lubéron in the mid 1800s. The trees flourished — as did the insects and mushrooms which arrived with them. A nature trail with information panels tells you more about the wealth of flora and fauna on the massif.

Start out at the parking area: follow the road behind the barrier preventing access to the Route des Crêtes, the narrow tarmac road on the crest of the Petit Lubéron; it is only open to walkers and cyclists. Almost at once, turn left onto the signposted *Sentier botanique*

This walk skirts the base of a limestone edge, the Roque des Bancs. Caves in this part of the Lubéron have been used as hideouts for centuries, most recently by the Maquis. Above the edge you can just see the tops of some cedars on the Route des Crêtes. While walking, have a look at the tops of the cedars: the youngsters have conical tops; the 'old men', who have already played the role of seed-sower, have flat tops.

(blue waymarks). Descend gently through cedars and then *garrigues*. In spring watch out for pockets of bright-white star-of-Bethlehem (*Ornithogalum umbellatum*) and the slender stalks of the rock sainfoin (*Hedysarum saxatile*), capped by a pyramid of pale pink florets. In about **30min**, at the bottom of the valley (spot height 628m), you come to flat area where holm oak from these slopes used to be smouldered into charcoal. At the fork here go right uphill on a stony path (this is the only noticeable climb in the walk). Another fork comes up five minutes later: these two paths quickly rejoin, but take the left-hand fork; it's easier going. Just after these paths rejoin, you come to another fork: go right uphill, passing signpost N° 6. At the next fork, seven minutes later, climb left uphill to a plateau. This ancient pastureland is no longer grazed and has been invaded by box, like so many other upland areas we visit. In **55min** come to a splendid viewpoint over the Durance Valley, with the Montagne Ste-Victoire visible to the left and the Alpilles to the far right (information panel N° 8).

From the viewpoint head north on a stony track. Soon a blue peg with an arrow sends you in a curve to the right and you rejoin the Route des Crêtes in 10 minutes. Turn left and follow it to a water tank on the left bearing the number 41 (**1h15min**). Head left off the road here, on a footpath waymarked with blue flashes (ignore a path off to the right almost at once). When you come to a fork in about seven minutes, turn right (blue arrow), immediately coming to the limestone edge shown on page 83. Perfectly smooth and bare, it clasps the slope like a girdle. An exceptionally pretty, shady path, where wild flowers and junipers join the oaks, takes you alongside this escarpment. A shepherds' shelter (*bergerie*) sprawling in ruins under an overhang of rock on the right (**1h40min**) is a sheltered sun trap — a good picnic spot on cool days. Three minutes past the *bergerie* go right at a fork and 10 minutes later meet the Route des Crêtes; turn right back to your car (**2h25min**).

Walk 5: DENTELLES DE MONTMIRAIL

Distance: 6km/3.7mi; 3h25min   See also photographs pages 7, 84

Grade: moderate-strenuous, with a total ascent of 350m/1150ft and a corresponding descent (sometimes on steep and stony paths). *Sure-footedness and agility required,* but the paths are not vertiginous.

Equipment: walking boots, sunhat, picnic, water

How to get there: 🚗 to the Col du Cayron (large parking area). From Gigondas follow LES FLORETS, DENTELLES DE MONTMIRAIL (Car tour 3). 1.3km along, the road reverts to track: continue ahead for another 0.7km and park at the col, just over 2km from the turn-off. Or 🚌 to Gigondas and walk to the col (add 4km/1h15min return)

Short walk: Col du Cayron — Rocher du Midi — Col du Cayron (2km/1.3mi; 1h40min; moderate climb/descent of 220m/720ft, *requiring agility;* equipment and access as above). Follow the main walk for 25min, then return to the three-way signpost and descend left to the Rocher du Midi (🏠). There turn right on the track to the col.

O ne of the most exquisite walks you will ever take, *anywhere,* this magnificent hike leads you up, over and between the Dentelles and their glistening vineyards — with splendid views to Mont Ventoux.

Start out at the Col du Cayron: climb the signposted SENTIER D'ACCES NORD AUX DENTELLES SARRASINES. From here until you reach the Col d'Alsau, put your faith in the blue dots; the path is *very* well waymarked. In under **20min** you come to a three-way signpost, where the Rocher du Midi *(Short walk)* is signposted to the right.

You climb quickly to the ridge atop the Dentelles Sarrasines, shown here. Then you follow the ridge west past a stupendous array of jagged rock, pierced with 'windows'. Beyond the Col d'Alsau, you head east again, above vineyards, between the Sarrasines on your left and the Grand Montmirail on your right.

Go straight uphill for COL D'ALSAU. Five minutes later you are in the setting shown on page 85. *(Here the Short walk returns to the signpost.)* Turn right along the undulating ridge, rounding the Rocher du Turc with its 'window' (626m/2050ft, the highest point in the Dentelles). At **45min** a signpost indicates a *very difficult* path back to the Rocher du Turc; ignore it; keep ahead beneath the 'window' of the Tête Vieille. Soon the descent begins (often on all fours). Drop down to the pine-scented Col d'Alsau at **1h05min** and turn left.

After 50m/yds turn up left for CANTON DU CLAPIS (blue waymarks), ignoring the track right to the Tour Sarrasine. At a Y-fork almost immediately, climb steps to the right (blue *and yellow* waymarks). The climb quickly levels out, as you skirt the Grand Montmirail on your right. *Now you must* **assiduously** *follow sparse* **but crucial yellow** *waymarks.* Make for the 'needle' of rock (Lame du Clapis) ahead in the valley: just as you approach it, clamber left over bedrock (waymarked). Beyond here, bear in mind that you must cross to the far side of the valley *before* it becomes a gorge. Watch for the waymarks (near a scree) taking you *very steeply* down to the left in hairpins; there is only one crossing point (**2h**) — in a very pretty setting of rock pools.

Soon the pine-scented path heads east towards a 'sugar loaf' hill of swirling rock, where you can see the Chapelle St-Christophe. Cross two streams; beyond the second you must clamber up bedrock (waymarked) and then struggle steeply up to a lane (**2h30min**). Turn right and, at a bend, climb the path up left to the beautifully-sited chapel (**2h40min**; photograph page 7). Then return to the lane and turn right. Beyond the Cassan *domaine*, at a fork (spot height 277; **2h55min**), go left through vineyards, back to the Col du Cayron (**3h25min**).

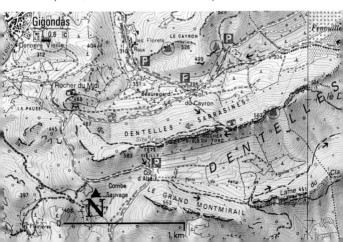

Walk 6: PONT DU GARD

See also photograph pages 46-47

Distance: 10.5km/6.5mi; 3h

Grade: fairly easy, with ascents totalling under 200m/650ft; avoid at weekends and holidays, when the crowds make walking on (or in) the aqueduct unbearably claustrophobic.

Equipment: stout lace-up walking shoes (walking boots preferable), sunhat, picnic, water, swimming things

How to get there: 🚗 to the large parking area on the right bank of the Gard (follow PONT DU GARD; RIVE DROITE; Car tour 4). Or 🚌 to Bégude de Vers-Pont-du-Gard. From the bus stop walk to the bridge, cross it, and continue to the car park where the walk starts (add about 20min each way).

Short walk: Rive Droite and Rive Gauche (3.5km/2.2mi; 1h15min; easy, with very little climbing; equipment and access as above). From the car park walk towards the Pont du Gard, then take the narrow lane passing under it. Follow the main walk from the 1h20min-point to the 1h45min-point. Then just turn down towards the left bank of the river and follow the nature trail for as long as you like before returning to the car park or bus stop.

For us it would be sacrilege to include the Pont du Gard only as part of a car tour — somewhere to stop for a short time, read what the guide books have to say, take a picture or two, and then move on. This colossal work of art (see pages 46-47) should be admired from all angles, and in different lights. So ideally spend a day here, lazing on the riverbank, picnicking and watching the kayakers zipping past. If you're not into swimming, take a bit of exercise with an early morning or late afternoon walk, this pleasant leg-stretcher along both banks of the Gard.

Start out at the large parking area on the right bank, near the tourist information office. Walk back towards Remoulins, to a large sign for 'Chez Fernand' on the left. Just past here turn right uphill on a footpath (yellow waymarks on a tree and a rock). A short climb of 100m/330ft follows, under a shady bower brightened by bird-song and wild flowers. After 2km (**50min**) you meet a crossing track (spot height 121m). Here you pick up the GR6 which has ascended from St-Bonnet: turn right and continue the slight climb. If you hear engines roaring, the racket comes from a moto-cross to the south, which fortunately does not come into view.

On coming to a crossing track, follow the GR waymarks down to the right. The trees along this *Cistus*-lined cart track have been cut back to permit views over Castillon-du-

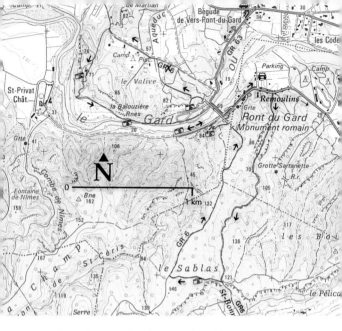

Gard in the north, the Gard Valley and, later on, the bridge itself. Pass some vestiges of the aqueduct on your right and then enter a tunnel. On leaving it, *ignore* both the GR waymarks (the GR crosses the bridge here) *and* the path on the left indicating 'Panorama 200m'. Instead descend to the road (**1h20min**).

Turn right and then go left on the narrow lane which runs under the bridge. Follow this for about 0.5km — or until you are convinced that your views of the bridge from the banks below could not possibly improve! Then return towards the aqueduct. About 50m/yds before you would pass beneath it again, turn right up a path (PANORAMA 200M is painted on a rock here). As you zigzag uphill, watch for a path on the right after about five minutes, to AQUEDUC PHOTO. This leads to a dramatic viewpoint over the bridge and river. Then continue uphill, coming to the top level of the aqueduct. If you are agile and have a head for heights, you can cross on the top (everyone does, although this is now officially prohibited). If you suffer from vertigo, you'll join Pat in the gloom of the claustrophobic water channel. After crossing,

Looking back to St-Bonnet-du-Gard from the sunny cart track where the GR6 joins the walk. The cart track followed on the left bank of the river is just as colourful.

descend the circular stairway (**1h45min**) and turn left following yet another PANORAMA 200M. Come to a fork and go left on a wider path. You approach a concrete marker showing the way to PANORAMA, to your left. From this look-out you can only see the bridge, not the river.

Return to the concrete marker just passed and follow it in the direction you were going before turning off to the viewpoint. You come to a wide earthen cross-path: turn left. You have rejoined the GR6, which has been rerouted in this area and is incorrectly drawn on the IGN map. Follow its red and white flashes past some substantial remains of the aqueduct (on your left) until you come to a road (under **2h**). Turn left here and pass a derelict camp site in three minutes. About eight minutes later, you pass a track turning back to the left. Turn left just *past* here, making for the electricity wires seen ahead. Soon you are heading towards some electricity poles rising from a rocky outcrop. After passing between these twin electricity poles, you have a splendid view across the river to the Château de St-Privat with its lovely gardens. Continue down this stony path (it curls down to the left just below the viewpoint).

The descent ends at a T-junction with another path, where you turn left. Edged by oaks and holly, this path eventually gives fine views to the river on the right. As you near the bridge, many trees and shrubs have been labelled, and benches are spread out along a pleasant *sentier botanique.* When you come to the bridge, cross it via the road and return to the parking area (**3h**).

Walk 7: LE DESTET • AUREILLE • LE DESTET

See also photographs pages 74, 92-93

Distance: 7.5km/4.7mi; 2h30min

Grade: easy (climbs of about 100m/330ft), but there is *no shade.*

Equipment: stout lace-up walking shoes, sunhat, water, optional picnic (or have lunch at Aureille)

How to get there: ➡ to Le Destet (southeast of St-Rémy, Car tour 5). From the junction of the D78 and D24 drive south towards Mouriès along the D24 and after 200m turn left on the first track you come to (one of the signposts here reads VALLEE DES BAUX). Continue uphill for about 0.8km and park off the side of the track when you are level with the far end of the moto-cross circuit.

Short walk: Circuit through the olive groves (4.5km/2.8mi; 1h35min; grade/equipment/access as above). Follow the main walk for 40min, then turn right downhill. Pick up the notes again after the 1h35min-point, deducting 55min from the following times.

Silvery leaves glisten beneath a porcelain-blue sky, and the air shimmers with heat, as you walk to the pretty village of Aureille and then through olive groves typical of the Alpilles. Choose a cool day between October and May for this countryside ramble *in full sun.*

Start out by trudging east along the track where you parked. Ignore the tracks off right to the farm of Vaudoret (**5min, 15min**). We'll delve into the Vaudoret olive groves later in the walk. In under **20min**, at a three-way junction, take the middle track or the one on the left (they rejoin); the track on the right is our return route. Four minutes later, ignore a track left uphill but, three minutes further on, at a Y-fork, *do* go left (and ignore a path off to the right a minute uphill). This track skirts to the right of a cultivated field, then brushes up against the cliffs we have been following since starting out. Notice the turpentine trees (*Pistacia terebinthus*), with their shiny leaves and clusters of reddish-brown fruits.

In about **35min** you reach a couple of buildings on the left; continue past them on a very overgrown grassy track. It loops away from the cliff wall and skirts a field

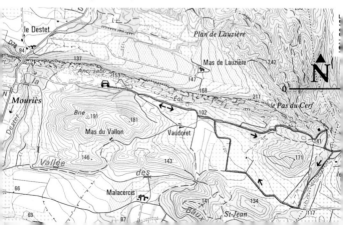

You cross olive groves brightened by gold grasses and hefty pink Scottish thistles. Once in a while the dark leaves of a fig or peach tree punctuate the landscape.

full of thistles. (The track is *very* faint here; keep to the left-hand side of the field; a stream is on your left.) On meeting a stronger crossing track, under four minutes past the buildings, turn left, crossing the stream. A minute later (**40min**), a strong track comes in from the left: ignore it; keep straight ahead. But notice, almost immediately, the good track down right into the olive groves — your return route. *(The Short walk goes right here.)*

Now ignore a track off to the right; continue ahead over a rushing watercourse. Keep ahead past another track off right, soon coming to a crest with a fine view ahead to Aureille, crowned by its castle. A beautiful rounded mountain with a tower rises behind the village: Les Opiès, the highest point in the Alpilles. Tar comes underfoot at a housing estate, where you join the GR6. When you come to a Y-fork, bear right on Rue du Batiment. Turn right to cross the pretty stream, and then go left towards the clock tower; a bar/café is just opposite (**1h05min**). Have a look at the unusual church before you leave Aureille.

Leave Aureille the way you came in (Rue du Batiment) and, at a Y-fork, keep right with the GR6 on the Chemin de St-Jean. When the tar ends (and the GR turns up right), note the time. Under 10 minutes later you will cross the rushing watercourse again. Just beyond it is your turn-off (left) into the Vaudoret olive groves (**1h35min**). Down in the heart of the groves, you meet a crossing track after 15 minutes: turn right into a quintessential Alpilles setting, with olive groves in the foreground and a backdrop of limestone cliffs. As the track curls round to the right, back towards the cliffs, the way is brighted by bright pinky-purple cranesbill (*Geranium tuberosum*) and Scottish thistles.

By **2h20min** you rejoin your outgoing route at the three-way fork; turn left here, back to your car (**2h30min**).

Walk 8: ST-REMY • LES BAUX • ST-REMY

See also photographs on pages 34-35, 36, 74

Distance: 13km/8mi; 4h

Grade: moderate, with climbs totalling 200m/650ft. The walk mostly follows tracks which are stony underfoot. Some agility is needed for the narrow path on the approach to Les Baux. The walk is not recommended in hot weather; there is virtually no shade en route.

Equipment: stout lace-up walking shoes (walking boots preferable), sunhat, long-sleeved shirt, long trousers, picnic, plenty of water. Note: you can get food and drink at Les Baux (halfway through the walk).

How to get there: 🚗 to the large parking area at the lake near St-Rémy. Follow the D5 south out of St-Rémy (Car tour 5). Note the km reading when you pass the tourist office (on your left); 0.5km further on, turn right for LE BARRAGE, as indicated by a small signpost. Park at the lake (Barrage des Peiroou) at the end of this road, 2km further on. Or 🚌 to Les Baux and do the circuit from there (the 1h45min-point in the walk). Also accessible by 🚌 to St-Rémy, but you will have to add an extra 6km/1h45min from there to the lake and back.

Short walks:

1 St-Rémy — Les Baux (5.5km/3.4mi; 1h45min; access/equipment as above). Grade as above, but the climb is under 150m/500ft. Follow the main walk to Les Baux and from there catch a bus back to St-Rémy (add up to 3km/45min to walk on to your car) or ask the tourist office in Les Baux to telephone for a taxi, to take you back to the lake.

2 Les Baux — St-Rémy (9km/5.6mi; 2h15min; easy). Use the notes for Car tour 5, page 37, to park at the viewing table near Les Baux. Follow the walk from the 2h30min-point to the end, then walk on from the lake to the D5 and follow it to the tourist office in St-Rémy, where they can advise on buses or call you a taxi. If you pre-arrange for a taxi to meet you at the lake, reckon on 6.5km/4mi; 1h30min.

This delightful walk is probably the most popular in the Alpilles, and deservedly so: it's not too long or too steep, and it leads from a gorgeous lake to one of the most famous beauty spots in France, the magnificently-sited citadel of Les Baux, shown on pages 34-35. Les Antiques (photograph page 36) and Glanum are close to the lake where the walk begins and ends, so plan to spend the whole day in this area.

Start out at the lake, the Barrage des Peiroou, much favoured by picnickers and anglers. Ignore the track closest to the lake. Locate the red and white flashes of the GR (there should be a small sign here on a tree: SENTIER GR6) and follow the GR uphill through pines on an earthen track. In two minutes

Cultivated fields spread below bare, bright-white limestone outcrops: this typical Alpilles landscape is characteristic of Car tour 5 and Walks 7 and 8.

you cross the road to the lake. Now take the stony track opposite; it bears a GR waymark. After 12 minutes, a path waymarked in yellow goes off to the left: ignore it; follow the track round to the right. At just over **15min** reach a tarred area where there is a water point (spot height 209m). Continue straight ahead along the tar, ignoring a track descending to the right. Looking left now, you'll see the huge ORTF relay equipment on the bluff of La Caume.

Ignore a path to the right and then two tracks going off to the left (not shown on the map); keep on the main track, which bends sharply to the right. You enjoy good views to the north, before the track turns southwards again. At this point (**30min**; spot height 266m) the main track continues ahead, but we fork right uphill on a footpath with both red and white GR waymarks and a yellow waymark. (This footpath gives super views of the north from a crest. If you prefer to avoid the climb, or if a mistral is blowing, stay on the track and fork right when you come to a T-junction almost at once.) So far the ascent has been imperceptible, but now we *do* climb. In about six minutes we reach the top with its fine views and gale-force winds. Five minutes later we're back down on the main track. Continue southwest along the main track now, ignoring a minor cart track going off to the right. Two minutes along ignore a track ('A143') coming in from the left and then a track off right to the fire watch-tower (Tour de Guet); continue straight ahead.

Now we are going to part company with the GR and take a much more attractive path. This path is *not way-marked*, so follow the notes carefully. Five minutes past the track up to the watch-tower (**55min**) the main track describes a deep U-bend, and you come to a junction of paths and tracks: a path comes down from the watchtower on the right, and another path goes out left to a triangulation point. Leave the main track here (it is the return route): take the track to the left of the main track, but to the right of the path to the triangulation point. You are walking parallel with the main track, but descending. After about 100m/yds downhill, turn left on another track — the first one you come to. Now you're heading in the direction of the triangulation point, and soon the track becomes a lovely grassy foot-path. Not far along, a path comes down from the trian-gulation point and joins you from the left.

After descending for about 15 minutes (**1h15min**) meet a wide stony crossing path with GR waymarks and turn left on it. In two minutes go round a chain barrier, then meet another track and turn right, coming to a first house. Here swing round to the left and climb between fruit trees on your left and giant yellow cineraria *(Senecio)*; you are approaching the cliffs below Les Baux. As you climb, look over to the left, where flat squared-off fields edged by bright limestone hills shimmer under the mauve-blue heat haze so typical of Provence. At about **1h30min** you reach the first of the massive bauxite mines. Before you walk ahead to inspect them, locate your ongoing path, which takes off

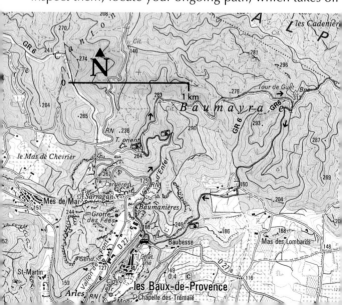

left about 50m/yds before the first mine, just behind a huge blade of rock on your left (well waymarked).

Return from the mine to the blade of rock and put on your long-sleeved shirt and long trousers. Turn right down the narrow path; it's hemmed in by holly oak and other spiny bushes. The path has been built up from layers of rocks (rather like a low stone wall), and some agility is needed to hop from one rock to another. Look left again for another typical Provençal landscape near Baubesse and the D27: silvery olive groves studded with sombre black cypresses. The ruined castle, from where Raymond de Turenne hurled his victims into the ravine on the left, is just above you now. In **1h45min** the path drops you down to the D27A. Turn right uphill to the parking area and walk past the parking attendant's stone kiosk (where the bus also stops). Up on your left, before you come to entrance to the village, is a shop selling snacks and drinks — a great pit stop on a hot day, especially if you don't want to join the midday crowds at the citadel.

From the shop walk back downhill past the parking attendant's kiosk and, when you are back on the D27A, turn left downhill following FONTVIEILLE and ARLES. When you reach the D27 go right, ignoring the left turn for Fontvieille and Arles. Soon you pass the Cathédral des Images and yet more mines. Now leave the GR: just beyond the sign denoting the exit from Les Baux (**2h 05min**), turn right on a track and walk to the right of a chain barrier (prohibiting vehicles). After climbing for less than 15 minutes, come to a T-junction with a stony track and turn left, still climbing (here you join a route waymarked in yellow). Three minutes uphill you round a bend and have a most magnificent view over to the left, across the Val d'Enfer and to Les Baux: the old mines are in foreground on other side of valley, with the village and the citadel behind them. The gentle Vallon de la Fontaine spreads out to the right of the citadel. Some 25 minutes off the D27 meet a tarmac road and cross straight over: climb the steep path opposite to the viewing table (*table d'orientation*; **2h30min**). Unless it is very hazy, you will have good views of the Camargue and the Rhône Valley, the Lubéron and Mont Ventoux. *Short walk 2 starts here.*

From the *table d'orientation* walk down the wide track. Join the tarmac road but, where it swings right, back towards Les Baux, go straight ahead on a tarmac lane, behind a chain barrier. Stalwart yellow mullein blooms here in summer. Five minutes along, at a Y-fork, ignore the concreted fire point up to the right; keep left along the track (white arrows). Ten minutes later, below spot height 276, beware: *ignore* the overgrown track on the right (waymarked with yellow arrows); *keep left* on the main track, even though a yellow 'X' indicates 'wrong way'.

Half an hour from the *table d'orientation* (**3h**; just beyond the point where the GR6 descends to the right), you rejoin your outgoing route, when you round the U-bend below the fire watch-tower. Five minutes later pass the track up to the watch-tower and two minutes after that the path you descended from the ridge-top viewpoint; keep right along the track here. Three minutes later, where a fainter track goes downhill to the right, keep left on a level track. It curls around to offer a superb view of the Alpilles and La Caume. Three minutes later pass the path you climbed to the ridge-top viewpoint, now on your left. Follow the track in a curve to the right. You come to a rock cutting (spot height 266; if you turn down left here, you can descend along your outgoing route, saving about 15-20 minutes).

The main walk continues past the cutting. Looking down left through the trees, soon you will spot the lake where you set out, with the spire of St-Rémy's church behind it. Ignore any grassy tracks downhill either side of the main track. The downhill track you want comes up about 20 minutes past the cutting (**3h40min**) — only about 150m/yds short of the D5. Look ahead through the pines on the left, and you'll see large white arrows pointing you downhill (along fire route A38; fire route A7, which you have been following, now continues ahead to the D5). Turn left downhill on this pine-shaded but stony track. On reaching the tarmac road to the lake, turn right downhill to your car (**4h**).

Walk 9: DIGUE A LA MER

See also photograph page 44
Distance: 7.5km/4.7mi; 2h15min

Grade: easy, level walk along stony tracks. But flat walks along blinding-white tracks where there is no shade can be surprisingly tiring. We would not recommend any walks longer than 2-3 hours in the Camargue. Rent a cycle instead!

Equipment: trainers, sunhat, sunglasses, suncream, long-sleeved shirt, long trousers, binoculars, plenty of water, optional picnic (any food attracts swarms of insects). *Adequate sun protection is mandatory; the cool breeze is deceptive, and sunstroke is a real possibility.*

How to get there: 🚌 to the pumping station between the Etang du Fangassier and the Etang de Galabert (accessible from Villeneuve on the D37 — the 146km-point in Car tour 6; see page 43). A sign here warns you not to leave anything of value visible in the car. Note also that outside winter months the car will be a furnace on your return.

This circuit on the north side of the Etang de Galabert is a good introduction to the Camargue, one of the very few places in the Mediterranean where flamingoes breed. Not only will you see your fill of flamingoes (45,000 individuals have been recorded here), but a great many other birds as well.

Start out at the pumping station between the Galabert and Fangassier lagoons. (The flamingoes breed on an islet in the Fangassier Lagoon, and from April to July their raised conical nests are under round the clock surveillance by the park and reserve authorities.) Follow the dyke (Digue à la Mer) northwest; the pump will be just on your left as you set off — churning away, with any luck. The lighthouse (Phare de la Gacholle) glimmers in the distance. Spiny glassworts (*Salicornia* species) predominate, peppered by the odd wizened-up

In May and July a magnificent colony of yellow sneezeworts flowers on the sand-bar. The lighthouse is in the far distance, hidden in haze.

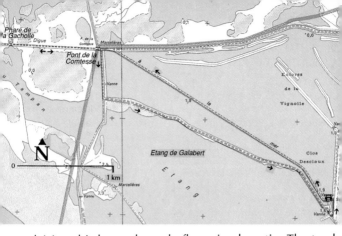

daisies, thistles and purple-flowering knautia. The track is embedded with tiny, perfectly-formed sea shells. A fairly stagnant strip of water is on your left and a narrow sand-bar beyond it; this will be the return route. The muted pinks and purples in the still water and the dull greens and yellows of the surface algae create beautiful abstract patterns. By the side of the path an intermittent double row of wooden piles helps to shore up the dyke; a sludge of salty foam clings to them. The monotony is broken only by the screeching of myriad seagulls swirling above an islet to the left. After **45min** you reach the Pont de la Comtesse, an important level-changing station. Cars are not allowed beyond this point, and walkers/cyclists are reminded to keep to the track. Passing the Etang du Tampan on the left, come to the lighthouse (**1h**), graced by a purple-flowering tamarisk, a fine specimen of the most characteristic tree in the Camargue. The surrounds are closed; it is inhabited.

Return to the Pont de la Comtesse and turn right on a wide track. Some 500m/yds along, be sure to turn left onto the sand-bar, not far beyond a barrier. (If you continue ahead, you would have to round the entire Etang de Galabert, a *very* long walk indeed.) This path, lined with gold grasses and sprouting huge yellow oyster plants with thistle-like leaves, runs down the middle of the sand-bar. While you wait for a flamingo to spread its black and salmon-red wings within camera range, be sure to watch your feet or you're likely to trip up on one of the hundreds of huge rabbit holes. Opposite 'shriek island', still swirling with gulls, you come across the colony of sneezeworts (*Achillea*) shown on page 97. When you approach the pumping station, turn right to cross a bridge; then, about 20m/yds beyond it, turn left on a track, back to your car (**2h15min**).

Walk 10: BERGERIE NEUVE • MONTCALMES • ST-GUILHEM OVERLOOK • BERGERIE NEUVE

Distance: 13.5km/8.4mi; 3h45min

Grade: easy-moderate, with a climb of 175m/575ft. The tracks used are *very* stony throughout, and there is virtually no shade en route.

Equipment: stout lace-up shoes (walking boots preferable), sunhat, picnic, water

How to get there: 🚗 to the Bergerie Neuve. Leave the D32 at the calvary on the south side of Puéchabon (Car tour 7): head west on the road here, then turn right immediately on a narrow tarred road. Follow it for 2km, until ends at a building (the *Bergerie Neuve*). Or 🚌 to Puéchabon and walk from there (add 6km/up to 1h30min return).

Short walk: Bergerie Neuve — Montcalmès — Bergerie Neuve (5km/3mi; 1h05min; easy climb of 85m/280ft; equipment/access as above). Follow the main walk for 35min and return the same way.

This walk across a limestone plateau (*causse*) above the Gorges de l'Hérault takes us through *garrigues* bristling with holm and holly oaks to the magnificent viewpoint over St-Guilhem-le-Désert shown on page 102. With each footstep we move back in time ... to the 8th century, when Charlemagne was on the throne.

The walk is sparingly waymarked with yellow flashes (and sometimes arrows). **Start out** at the Bergerie Neuve: take the motorable track furthest to the left and climb to the hamlet of Lavène (**15min**). Today there are only a couple of inhabited buildings spilling out window-boxes fresh with colour, but in the 8th century Lavène was a *cité*. Continue on the main track, following yellow waymarking and heading straight towards St-Baudille (with the large relay station), one of the peaks of the Séranne massif. Ten minutes along you pass a *lavogne* (a paved watering hole for animals) on the left-hand side of the track ('Lac Neuf' on the map). Just beyond it, leave the main track, which continues to the left. Go straight ahead, along a very stony track, to the ruined fortified hamlet of Montcalmès (**35min**). The huge château here also dates from the 8th century and was given by Charlemagne to St-Benoit. The very substantial remains include walls, arches, doorways, and a very well-preserved *bergerie* and baking oven. There is

The church of St-Sylvestre-des-Brousses, dating from the 12th century, rises above vineyards near the end of the walk.

Baking oven at the ruined château of Montcalmès, an excellent spot to end the Short walk with a picnic.

shade here, and grass; it makes a superb picnic spot where you can end the Short walk. Be sure to explore the remains *carefully;* some of the masonry is unstable.

Continuing on the track, in under 10 minutes you pass a second, semi-circular *lavogne* on the right ('Le Laquet'). Now St-Baudille and the mountains behind St-Guilhem appear very close indeed. Five minutes past the *lavogne* ignore a track off to the left. A minute later, ignore a second track off left; keep on the main track, which bears right. The track then heads obliquely left, passing masses of small rock quarries, to get to the western edge of the plateau (**1h10min**), from where the view towards the Séranne improves.

Now the track curves to the left and heads southwest in a straight line. Leave it here: locate the small marker-stone on your right, waymarked with a yellow flash. This indicates a narrow footpath to the right which skirts the edge of the plateau. Keep an eye out for the turpentine and mastic trees (*Pistacia terebinthus* and *Pistacia lentiscus*), growing amidst the holm and holly oaks. Their red-to-black berries feed the birds that winter here. In **1h35min** you reach the TV relay above St-Guilhem, with its noisy wind-powered generator. Turn right to savour the exquisite view shown on page 102. St-Guilhem lies far below, a river of salmon-coloured rooftops flowing through the Combe de Gellone, below the menacing cliffs of the Cirque de l'Infernet. The abbey church is clearly visible.

Take the track leading away from the relay. In five minutes you pass a deep pit on your left. Two minutes later, join the main track and go right, coming to a water tank on your right in three minutes (spot height 279m). Turn left here: the only waymark is a yellow arrow coming *in* to your route *from* the left. (*The track*

100

straight ahead is an alternative, equally atttractive route, indicated by red dots on the map above.) In five minutes come to a T-junction; turn right (yellow arrow). A minute later ignore a track off right. Soon you look back over to the ruined hamlet of Montcalmès, through clearings in the scrub. Some 20 minutes after leaving the water tank (**2h05min**) you meet a first *clear* track going off to the right: ignore it; it bears a yellow 'X'. Ignore another track on the right just a minute later (it rejoins the first track). But four minutes later, when you are almost back to the *lavogne* on your outgoing route, turn right on a very stony track marked with a yellow flash and a cairn. It rises slightly before descending steeply. There are fine views south to Aniane and the Hérault once you have cleared the trees and are approaching a vast spread of vineyards.

At **2h50min** you reach the pink-roofed chapel shown on page 99, St-Sylvestre-des-Brousses. Like the abbey church at St-Guilhem, this was an important stop along the pilgrims' route to Santiago de Compostela. Head left downhill on the track behind the chapel. *(Or, if you came by the alternative route, keep straight ahead* *downhill.*) The track then climbs to a crossing track, from where Puéchabon is visible to the right (**3h10min**). Turn left and keep climbing gently, now following *red* waymarks. When you rejoin the little lane to the *bergerie*, turn left back to your car (**3h45min**).

View over St-Guilhem from the plateau. The rounded apse of the abbey church (all that remains of the original monastery founded by St-Guilhem) is clearly visible. The church still displays its most precious relic — a piece of the true cross, given by Charlemagne to his friend Guilhem when the monastery was founded in 804.

Walk 11: SOURCE OF THE VIS

See also photographs pages 12-13 and 50-51

Distance: 11km/6.8mi; 2h40min

Grade: fairly easy, with climbs totalling only about 100m/350ft. But some agility is required, and you will need to use hands and feet in a few places.

Equipment: stout lace-up shoes (walking boots preferable), sunhat, picnic, water, swimming things

How to get there: 🚌 to Navacelles (Car tour 8). Park near the *auberge*.

Short walk: Navacelles — River Vis — Navacelles (4km/2.5mi; 1h10min; grade, equipment, access as above). Follow the main walk for about 35min and return the same way.

This walk is perfect for a hot day; there's some shade en route, and the surging source of the river Vis at the end of the walk is blissfully cooling. This crystal-clear river is also an ideal swimming-hole, so take a picnic and plan to spend much of the day by its banks.

Start out at the *auberge*. Cross the road to the post box, where there is a GR waymark on the wall ahead. Make for the river but, when you see the bridge ahead, don't walk to it: fork left uphill on a tarmac path. You pass the church on the right and continue uphill on a narrow lane. Pass to the right of a rounded wall bearing a yellow waymark. Then, when you come to the road, turn right. This slog up tarmac is unpleasant in hot weather, but in only about **10min** you come to the top of the climb, at a crossroads. Here the D130 goes left to St-Maurice and the D713 ahead to Blandas. In between them is a path marked with a green arrow and a signpost indicating that the source of the Vis is 1h away (for the *very* fleet of foot!).

Follow the path; it's marked with blue paint and leads you gently downhill past bright yellow broom, which flowers from April to July. In **20min** pass above a dam, beyond which the undulating path narrows. Sometimes you are quite high above the river so, although the drop is not sheer, watch your footing. Various bell-flowers are among the flora brightening this shady bower. In **30min** you descend very steeply to a T-junction with another path, where you turn left.

This is a lovely earthen path, pleasantly free of stones underfoot. The river is singing over on your right and, a minute along, you join it at a grassy verge, a fine picnic spot. But before you settle for the day, continue just a short way further — to another gorgeous spot, where flat slabs of rock jut out into the river. This is an ideal spot to launch yourself for a swim and sunbathe afterwards. Damsel- and dragonflies in fluorescent hues dart about here, vying with the cornflower blue, orange, and yellow butterflies for attention; but most spectacular are the moths, their wings an intricate pattern of scarlet, teal blue and black. Until you reach the source, this is the most beautiful part of the walk.

Soon the path is somewhat overgrown and climbs away from the river. At just over **1h05min** you pass the abandoned farmhouse of Les Pujols on the right. (On cool days, this open area makes a pleasant sun-trap for a picnic.) A magnificent cedar forest comes into view on the opposite riverbank ten minutes later. (A *circuit botanique* signposted from the D713 descends to the source through this forest; see Car tour 8 and dotted red lines on the map.) In **1h20min** turn right downhill on a path marked with a cairn (you won't see any paint waymarks until you have started down it). It's a steep descent of a couple of minutes to the mill, from where you'll have to scramble for another minute to enjoy the view of the source shown below. The atmosphere in this green cauldron is wonderfully invigorating.

As you climb back up from the source, the enormous cliffs of the Causse du Larzac tower above you. In 35 minutes you will be back at the place where rocks jut out into the river. Just past the grassy verge, be sure to climb uphill to the right on your outgoing path; there *are* waymarks here, but they are easily missed. (The path straight ahead, indicated on the map by red dots, leads to a ford over to the dam passed earlier and then a track out onto the road, but the river can only be forded in summer.)

In **1h25min** you should be back at the road junction. If you are staying overnight in Nava-

The Vis surges through a ruined 18th-century mill at its source. Incredibly, this torrent suddenly ceased in April 1776. One can imagine the fear of the local populace — who not only depended upon the Vis, but upon the mighty Hérault, which it feeds. Eight days later, as inexplicably as it had ceased, the source boiled over its cauldron again.

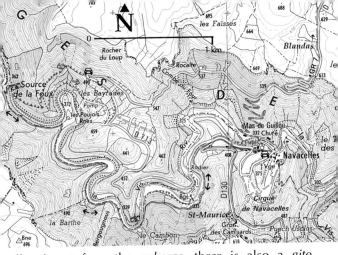

celles (apart from the *auberge*, there is also a *gîte d'étape*), and you do this walk late in day, you'll come back into the village hugging yourself with the knowledge that you have this whole magnificent amphitheatre *almost* all to yourself. High up to the right, on the plateau, you can spot the farm of Baume-Auriol, from where you probably first saw the *cirque*. When the road curves round, and the statue on the hillock in the 'moat' is just ahead of you, turn down the tarred lane that you climbed at the start of the walk. As you descend, don't fail to notice the ingenious door knockers. At **2h40min** you're back at the *auberge*.

Walk 12: MALAVIEILLE • LE CASTELLAS • LA LIEUDE • MALAVIEILLE

Distance: 13km/8mi; 3h10min

Grade: easy-moderate, with an overall climb of 300m/1000ft. Some agility is required on the approach to and descent from the *castellas*, where you may have to use your hands. Good surfaces underfoot, but virtually no shade.

Equipment: stout lace-up shoes (walking boots preferable), sunhat, long-sleeved shirt, long trousers, picnic, water

How to get there: 🚗 to Malavieille (Car tour 9). Follow MERIFONS on the D8E between Octon and Salasc; Malavieille is 1.3km beyond the turn-off. Go straight through the village, then continue on a narrow tarmac road and park on the right, 0.6km past the sign for Malavieille. Or 🚐 to Octon and walk from there (add 4km/2.5mi; 1h *each way*).

Short walk: La Lieude — Le Castellas — La Lieude (1.5km/1mi; 1h; equipment/grade as above, with a climb and descent of 150m/500ft). Access as above, but park at La Lieude, 2.2km beyond Malavieille.

This exceedingly beautiful walk is also interesting from a geological point of view. We cross a landscape of *ruffes* (see caption opposite) and climb a 'thimble' of basalt, recalling the volcanic origins of the

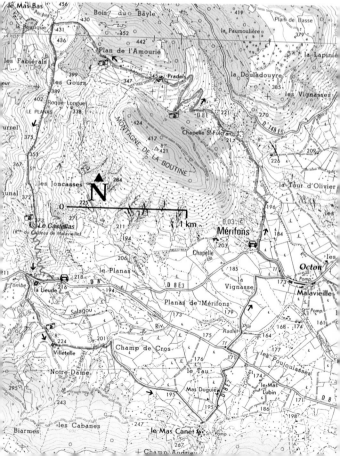

Looking south along the Rieupeyre Valley to the silhouette of the 'castellas' (ruined Château de Malavieille) in the distance. This area, near Lake Salagou, is renowned for its 'ruffes' — furrows of clay-bearing limestone soil. The striking contrast between the spring-green grass and this red soil is one of the highlights of the walk.

area. Embedded in this burgundy-red soil are fossilized animal prints dating from the Primary Era.

From the parking area **start out** by heading north along the red earthen track (green flash waymarks). On coming to a fork, go half left; don't continue straight ahead (a green flash is painted on a meter at ground level). The track is encrusted with pale grey-green lichen and stonecrop. You descend into a little valley and pass the ruins of a 15th-century chapel on the right (**15min**); it is dedicated to St-Fulcran, the patron saint of Lodève. Keep straight ahead past the chapel, at first following electricity wires.

In **20min** the way curves left up an old stone-laid trail, to mount the flanks of the Montagne de la Boutine. As you climb in deep zigzags there are fine views of the plain below, especially the vineyards in the southwest (where the photograph on page 57 was taken). In **40min** you arrive at Pradels, a honey-coloured huddle of stone houses. Leave it on a narrow concrete lane, continuing along the mountainside. Soon you enjoy the view shown above: you look straight down the deep Rieupeyre Valley to the silhouette of the *castellas* on the far side. In spring the lime-green hillsides are smothered with bright yellow broom.

The highest point of the walk is reached in **1h**. From here (spot height 431) you look out right to Le Mas Bas and Brenas, rising from a patchwork quilt of fields. Turn left (green arrow) and descend due south towards the *castellas* on another lane (the road continues to Le Mas Bas). The concrete gives way to a delightful grassy trail. Look to your left now: on the far side of the Rieupeyre Valley, wine-red *ruffes* stream vertically down the hillsides through the broom, almost like lava flows.

At **1h20min** pass a barn on right and come upon a cultivated field. Don't cross the field; walk along the left-hand edge of it and then curve round to the right. Now locate the *very clear* earthen path to the ruins, on your left (be sure to find it, or you will end up lacerated by brambles). Scramble up into the ruins (**1h35min**) and enjoy the panorama and your picnic lunch.

On the very steep, stony descent (you may need to use your hands) watch for the waymarks indicating the best footholds. You descend to a shelter housing the fossilised imprints of *Thereapsides*, precursors of mammals. They lived in this area, where there is thought to have been a watering-hole, some 250 million years ago (a long time before the dinosaurs). They were probably furry and warm-blooded. The prints are hard to see at first, until you realise that these were *not* large animals. The largest of them was only about 3m/12ft long, the smallest 50cm/under 2ft, so the prints are quite small.

With your back to the shelter, head right along the road to La Lieude (**2h05min**). Just past the last house *on the left*, turn left down an earthen path (green waymark after a dozen paces). Cross a stream and go ahead on a two-wheeled track, crossing another bridge a minute later. A short climb follows: bear left at a fork (green waymark on a rock). From here there is a good view towards Lake Salagou and back to the ruins and the Rieupeyre Valley. Come to a T-junction and turn left (a farm building is on the right). At the next fork go right uphill (green arrow on a rock), heading between fields towards some cypresses.

On reaching Le Mas Canet (**2h45min**) turn left. At an intersection, where there is a cross on the right, continue straight ahead. Meet the D8: turn left towards BRENAS and OCTON, but after 200m/yds go right on a narrow tarmac lane (the first one you come to). Not long after crossing a concrete ford you reach Malavieille and turn left back to your car (**3h10min**).

Walk 13: CIRQUE DE MOUREZE

See also photograph page 11   **Distance:** 5.5km/3.4mi; 2h35min
Grade: easy-moderate, with an initial climb of 300m/1000ft. The paths in the *cirque* are very stony underfoot — ankle-twisting terrain. Some agility is needed. Little shade en route.
Equipment: stout lace-up shoes (walking boots preferable), sunhat, long-sleeved shirt, picnic, water
How to get there: 🚗 to Mourèze (Car tour 9). Or 🚌 to Mourèze.
Short walk: Explore the *cirque* (1h; grade/access/equipment as above).

Not only does this walk explore the extraordinary Cirque de Mourèze from all angles, but you enjoy the best possible view over the Lac du Salagou, one of the most famous beauty spots in Hérault.

Begin the walk opposite the bus shelter east of the church; follow DIRECTION DU CIRQUE along a tarred lane. Turn left towards the church at the first alley, and then turn right. After passing the last house, you come to a fork; the left-hand path (the return route) is signposted COL DE PORTES. Keep straight ahead (the right-hand fork). There are no waymarks here, but head for the large pillars of rock straight ahead. In **10min** you will find yourself in the rock chaos; by now you will have picked up blue flash waymarks. Follow them assiduously, bearing in mind that you want to head due north at first, to the foot of the mountain ahead, Liausson. You pass below one of the most famous rocks in the chaos, The Sphinx (photograph page 11), about five minutes later.

Liausson and the Lac du Salagou from the summit of Mount Liausson. On the right is Mont Redon, one of the three hills rising up from the lake. The lake is set in a landscape of 'ruffes' (see caption page 107).

Eventually the path veers to the right, edging towards the mountain. At about **35min** you come to a T-junction (spot height 317m). Ignore the old charcoal burners' path to the right; turn *left*. Some 20 paces up this path, a tree on left is waymarked with *red and blue* flashes; follow this new waymarking up the mountain. The path is fairly steep, but not very stony, and it is pleasantly shaded by holm oaks. You gain height quickly and easily, at the same time enjoying ever-improving views to the south over Mourèze and its *cirque,* the Pic de Vissou (with the transmitter), and the distant sea. Caroux and the Espinouse rise in the west.

The summit (523m/1720ft) is reached in **1h**, at the viewpoint shown on pages 108-109, with the Causse du Larzac and the Cévennes in the distance. From here head west along the crest, following *blue* waymarks. You pass to the right of the ruined priory of St-Jean d'Aureillian and then reach a second summit (535m; **1h20min**). This is a fine viewpoint over the dolomitic pillars in the *cirque* and the maze of blinding-white paths that wind through it. The (sometimes awkward) descent to the Col de Portes begins here. At a fork 15 minutes downhill be sure to go right (blue arrow); the path down to the left leads to some more interesting dolomitic formations, but is a cul-de-sac. (Allow *double* the time on the signposts, if you take these diversions!)

Reach the Col de Portes in **1h50min**; here arrows point in all directions. Turn down left to Mourèze. Ten minutes below the col come to a major junction, where two trees are surrounded by rocks, and a track goes off to the right. Turn down left here on a track (towards the Pic de Vissou). Then leave this track after just four minutes: go left on a footpath waymarked in blue (spot height 280m). It brings you back into the *cirque* just north of the ruined castle. Huge rock pillars soon tower above you, as you battle your way through a tall forest

of pungent broom. At **2h25min** you're back at the fork you first encountered at the start of the walk. Turn right to pass the church and return to your car (**2h35min**).

IGN 2643O

Walk 14: MONS • GORGES D'HERIC • MONS

See also photograph page 72   Distance: 14km/8.7mi; 5h20min
Grade: moderate-strenuous, with ascents totalling 600m/1970ft, of which 500m/1650ft at the outset. Excellent surfaces underfoot.

Equipment: stout lace-up shoes (walking boots preferable), sunhat, long-sleeved shirt, long trousers, picnic, water, swimming things. Snacks and drinks are available halfway through the walk, at Héric.

How to get there: 🚗 to Mons, above La Trivalle (Car tour 9); park near the church. Or 🚌 to La Trivalle, from where you must climb to Mons (0.8km/15min each way).

Short walks: Both start at the tourist office at Mons la Trivalle, where you board 'Le Petit Train' shown on page 72 for an excursion up the Gorges d'Héric (operates all year round). The train turns round halfway up the gorge, at the Gouffre du Cerisier; get off there. Arrange with the driver to be collected again when he makes a later run. Wear trainers and a sunhat; take picnic, water, swimming things.

1   Gouffre du Cerisier — Héric — Gouffre du Cerisier (7km/4.3mi; 2h; easy climb of 150m/500ft). Follow the concrete lane to the isolated mountain hamlet of Héric (snacks/drinks available). Then descend to the Gouffre du Cerisier for your return train.

2   Gouffre du Cerisier — Parking (3km/2mi; 1h; very easy descent on a concrete lane). From the Gouffre walk back down the gorge to the parking area, and pick up the train there for the return to La Trivalle.

Alternative route: Mons — Col du Roujas — Col de la Maure — Gorges d'Héric — Mons (13.5km/8.4mi; 5h40min; strenuous, with a total ascent of 650m/2130ft, *much of it a steep scramble over boulders;* access/equipment as main walk, but boots are mandatory). At the 30min-point follow blue waymarks, to clamber (sometimes on all fours) straight up the bed of the Ruisseau du Roujas. After about 1h you come to the Col du Roujas and a fantastic view across the gorge to the jagged peaks of the Cirque de Farrières on Caroux. From this col head left for COL DE LA MAURE, following *yellow* flashes. (These waymarks are hard to locate at first, but once you have found the correct path, it is very well waymarked and maintained.) This easy path takes you past a viewpoint with a cairn (on your left, 15min from the Col du Roujas), from where you look out over Mons and the Jaur Valley. Continue northeast on the path, through deep shade of chestnuts, until you come to a strong crossing path (45min from the col). This is the main walk route (*red* waymarks); turn right and follow the main walk from the 1h55min-point (it has taken you 20min longer).

Whether you do the short stroll from the Gouffre du Cerisier or you flounder up the chaotic Roujas riverbed, you can anticipate a glorious and rewarding day out. Your physical needs are catered for with plenty of shade, beautifully-surfaced paths underfoot, and a refreshment stop at Héric. Spiritually the walk is as fulfilling as a symphony, with lofty peaks piercing the clouds above you, an emerald-green river bouncing down beside you, and the trill of bird-song.

Start out at Mons church. Climb the narrow road just opposite it, heading up a narrow alley towards an arch. There are blue and white flashes on an electricity pole on the left. Go under the arch and turn left in front of the *gîte*, into another alley. Curve round to the right uphill (another blue/white flash on a pole) on a concrete lane. In just over **5min** you must leave this lane (there is a blue 'X' on a wall to your left and a shed/garage straight ahead of you here): turn up stone steps on your right, to begin climbing an old stone-laid trail waymarked in blue and red. Almost at once you pass a house on the left, with an interesting outdoor oven. If the owners of the house have scattered some belongings across the path, don't worry that you have stumbled into a private garden; just forge ahead. Three minutes past here the trail forks: go left up stone steps.

In **30min**, at a stream crossing, the red and blue routes part company. Go left, following the red flashes. *The Alternative 'walk' scrambles straight ahead up the steep streambed (copiously waymarked in blue).* The

This bridge over the Vialais (a tributary of the Héric) is crossed at 3h20min. It is an ideal picnicking and swimming spot. If you are only doing Short walk 1, you can reach this bridge in under 10 minutes from Héric by following the signpost to BARDOU.

The hamlet of Héric, below the Espinouse massif. Here, in the 'middle of nowhere', you can have a snack or drink on the tree-shaded terrace of the 'buvette'.

reason for the superb stone-laid trail is soon apparent: myriad walls and a broad-leafed canopy overhead testify to intensive cultivation of the chestnut tree in the past. If you come in early summer, when the berries have fallen to the ground and lie squashed in pools of black juice, you'll also notice the mulberry trees, with their oval, serrated leaves. Mulberry trees were introduced (especially around Ganges) as early as the 13th century, to develop the silkworm industry; the caterpillars fed on mulberry leaves.

At **1h55min** come to the Col de la Maure ('Col de Molle' on the IGN map). The Alternative walk comes in from the right here, by the path marked with cairns.* Continue uphill, in 10 minutes passing to the right of a rock where 'Col de Maure' is painted in red, indicating the way you have come. Soon you will see blue and red waymarks ahead — a good example of an over-abundance of waymarking, which only leads to confusion. At **2h25min** come to a fork at the Col du Renard and go right, following red flashes. The path to the left goes down to Bardou, but we pass above the hamlet.

At **2h35min** the GR7 comes up from the left (from Bardou). Turn right here, almost immediately coming to the Col de Bardou. Here a stony path goes ahead uphill; follow the GR downhill to the right, beneath more chestnuts. At **3h20min** you cross the Vialais stream, on the bridge shown opposite. When you come to a fork almost immediately after the bridge, turn left uphill, coming to another stream and a grassy verge.

At **3h30min** signposts announce the *buvette* at Héric and our ongoing path (to DOUCH). Handily, it leads straight through the outdoor terrace of this café. So stop awhile, under the flowering ash, the fig, or the false acacia. Then continue to the track on the far side of the terrace and turn right downhill (the GR7 climbs a path

*If you can spare another 1h30min return, follow this *easy, well-waymarked* path to the right, to the Col du Roujas. First you will pass a fine view over Mons and, from the Col du Roujas, you will have a tremendous view over the gorge and the jagged peaks of Caroux.

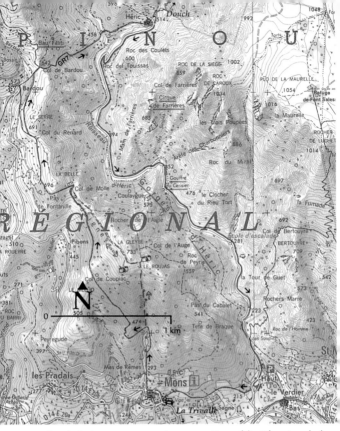

to the left here, to continue to Douch). The track becomes a concrete drive, and we amble down it for the next hour and a half. Some 30 minutes downhill, look straight up ahead at La Belle — a needle of rock. The Col de la Maure, where the main and alternative routes met, is just to left of it. Further down, the jagged, green-tinged peaks of the Cirque de Farrières ahead seem to cut off our ongoing route. Beyond a second bridge we come to the Gouffre du Cerisier, where a large pool on the right is fed by a lovely waterfall. The little 'train' shown on page 72 turns round here. About 15 minutes later pass below a climbing edge. Cross another bridge where a path heads left, to another superb rock pool.

At **5h** you leave the gorges. Walk straight ahead to a sign, 'parking municipal payant', then turn right uphill on a concrete path (passing a *gîte* called 'Le Caroux' on your right). The path, which skirts to the right of a vineyard, is fairly overgrown. Where a track comes up from the left, turn right uphill on a wider path, still beside vineyards on your left. In 15 minutes, at a T-junction in Mons, turn left downhill to the church (**5h20min**).

Walk 15: CIRCUIT ABOVE OLARGUES

See also photograph pages 54-55

Distance: 9km/5.6mi; 2h20min

Grade: fairly easy, with an initial ascent of 150m/500ft. All the tracks and paths are good underfoot.

Equipment: trainers or stout lace-up shoes, sunhat, picnic, water

How to get there: 🚌 to Olargues. Park in the parking area by the river, at the eastern end of the village (Car tour 9). Or 🚐 to Olargues.

This walk in the foothills of the Monts de l'Espinouse is both easy and rewarding. There are several fine viewpoints en route, but other corners of interest as well, like the delightful chapel of 'St Martin of the Eggs' shown below. The walk starts at Olargues, the medieval village shown on pages 54-55. It is dominated by an 11th-century bell-tower which crowns the dungeon of its old castle. The castle was taken by Simon de Montfort in 1210 during the crusades against the Cathars (see box page 63), but only destroyed under Louis XIII. You might like to climb the tower at the end of the walk, for its fine panorama, unimpeded by trees.

Olargues fulfils its promise of being 'one of the most beautiful villages in France', and there is no better view of its setting than that from the car park, where the ancient Pont du Diable (1202) spans the Jaur. This is where **the walk begins**. Cross the bridge leading to the D908 and turn right. You come at once to a Total petrol station. Turn left uphill on the narrow concrete road on the far side of the petrol station, climbing in a north-westerly direction up to the little valley of the Cesse. Vineyards stretch away to your left, and purple bell-flowers line the roadside. The route is waymarked in blue and soon festooned with cherry trees.

In **15min**, at a T-junction, bear right uphill in the direction of Caroux above the Gorges d'Héric (setting for Walk 14). Now following a track, you pass beside more vineyards, keeping them to the left. A gorgeous lone flowering ash makes a splash on the opposite side of the valley in early summer. Soon you're climbing through chestnuts as well as cherry trees and vines. At a

St-Martin-des-Oeufs is passed after about 40 minutes; its walls are decorated with charming frescoes.

fork met in **30min**, go right uphill. Five minutes later you are just opposite Mas du Gua. The bare rock edges of the Espinouse massif rise above you here, but it is always to the high rock escarpment beyond the Gorges d'Héric that the eye is drawn. When you come to a fork where there is a blue and white 'X' on the track to the right, go left. Now you will enjoy a fine view to the right over vineyards and eastwards along the valleys of the Jaur and Orb. The triangular peak at the far end of the valley is Tantajo, near Bédarieux (Car tour 9).

At about **40min** come to the tiny chapel of St-Martin-des-Oeufs on the right (photograph page 115). Just past this chapel, turn right to follow a grassy trail through a lovely chestnut wood, the Bois de Salan. Foxgloves brighten this shady bower in early summer. At just over **50min** come to a fork and bear right down into the Combe de Codouls. A small bridge is crossed and, two minutes later, you meet the concrete road from Les Sagnes: turn right downhill. Ignore roads and tracks coming in from the right, and soon enjoy a fine view straight ahead, towards the bell tower on its wooded knoll. When you come to Le Cros (**1h15min**), notice how the red roof tiles are weighted down with stones as a protection against the mistral. This largish hamlet also boasts a marvellous view over the Jaur Valley and Olargues. Five minutes later, in the lower part of Le Cros, you will hear rushing water. Don't go straight ahead; curve down in a U-turn to the left, into a pretty glen with a waterfall, and cross a bridge.

Some 300m/yds beyond the bridge, at **1h25min**, you come to a junction: turn right downhill, passing to the right of a modern stone building, carefully constructed in the traditional style. Straight ahead now, on the far side of vineyards, is the Prieuré de St-Julien (see photograph). On coming to a fork, go left on concrete, climbing slightly, before descending into a small ravine, from where there are fine views left — up to Caroux and along to where Tantajo punctuates the end of the valley. At another fork, where a dusty farm track goes left (**1h35min**), curve round on concrete, making a a U-turn to the right.

We descend back into Olargues through vineyards and cherry trees, looking east to the priory of St-Julien. On the right is the long valley of the Jaur and the Orb.

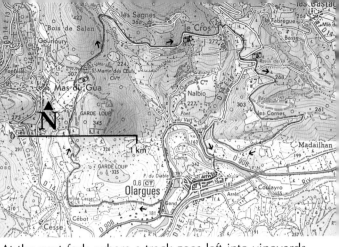

At the next fork, where a track goes left into vineyards, keep right as waymarked, soon coming onto concrete again. A three-way junction poses a bit of a problem now, since waymarks have disappeared: go left down-hill, ignoring the tracks straight ahead and to the right. Soon you are following electricity wires (on your right). From here the priory seems within arm's reach, as you walk through a plantation of firs.

Go right at the next fork, soon passing a cypress-studded cemetery on the left and walking straight towards the tower and red roofs of Olargues. Olive trees border this concrete lane. When you meet the the D14E, turn left downhill. Then cross the N908 and enter Olargues from the west. Now wander eastwards through the village (where some façades date from the 13th century), back to the car park (**2h20min**).

Walk 16: CIRCUIT ABOVE ST-PONS

Distance: 16km/10mi; 4h20min

Grade: moderate, with total ascents of 475m/1560ft. Some stony paths and tracks; very steep (but short) descent into St-Pons.

Equipment: stout lace-up shoes (walking boots preferable), sunhat, long-sleeved shirt, long trousers, picnic, water

How to get there: 🚌 to St-Pons. Park in the Place Forail, near the cathedral (Car tours 9, 10). Or 🚐 or 🚕 to St-Pons.

Short walk: D907 above Brassac — St-Pons (4.5km/2.8mi; 1h35min; easy, with a short, steep descent into St-Pons; equipment as above, but stout shoes will suffice). Ask friends to take you to the starting point or, on arriving in St-Pons, arrange for a taxi at the tourist office in the Place Forail. By car or taxi head north on the D907 for LA SALVETAT. About 0.8km past the turn-off left for Brassac watch for a track on the right between two stone pillars, signposted 'Camping Vert'. Start here by picking up the main walk at the 2h45min-point.

Frankly, this walk begins rather inauspiciously, with a hour's slog up a track. But beyond the Tailhos Valley, on the slopes of the Somail massif, you feel on top of the world. You pass through Brassac, an enchanting village, and then pick up the old 'road' from La Salvetat to St-Pons. This is the loveliest part of the walk, as you stride out across a ridge covered in gold grasses and summer-flowering purple heather.

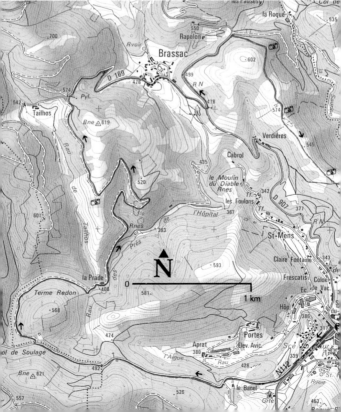

Start out at the Place Forail, the junction of the D907 and N112. Follow the N112 southwest (MAZAMET, CASTRES). This walk *used to be* waymarked with two yellow flashes. These waymarks have faded, so follow the route description carefully. Before you reach the Shell petrol station on the left-hand side of the N112, you come to a crossroads. Ignore both the left- and right-hand roads; go *half right* up the Route de Marthomis, climbing gently away from the N112. The surrounding slopes are thickly wooded but, on your right, across the Aigue Valley, the top of one of the hills (spot height 593m) is bald — a 'beacon' that is visible for much of the walk; in springtime it glows with yellow broom.

At **35min** ignore the track off to the right. Almost immediately afterwards, pass a cross on the right. The way flattens out now, and chestnuts arch over the road. At under **50min**, where the lane goes ahead to the Col de Soulage, turn right downhill on a track, heading back the way you came, passing to the right of a moto-cross and tree-felling area, both of which give a messy, patchy look to the hillsides. Ignore another track to the right; stay on main track, going downhill into the Tailhos Valley. On coming to a fork (**1h05min**) ignore the track straight ahead; turn down sharp left towards the river, on a grassy two-wheel track. Cross the bridge over the stream and come to the old stone buildings of La Prade, awash in a sea of white-flowering wild carrots in early summer. The stream rushes below on the right.

The walk is much prettier now, as you follow a side-valley on the right where, in springtime, fox-gloves add a touch of colour to the ubiquitous spruce and chestnuts. At **1h15min** bear left uphill at a fork (faded yellow flashes). Some 15 minutes later ignore a faint track to the right (below spot height 520m). Soon the Tailhos Valley opens up on your left, and the farm buildings of Tailhos are seen ahead. At **1h 50min** you climb out of the trees to an exhilarating, sunny plateau with

IGN 2444E

far-reaching views. At **2h05min** meet a road and turn right uphill. Then descend gently under chestnuts to Brassac (**2h20min**), where the church is off to the left. You pass a fine barn with buttresses and cross a stream.

From Brassac climb to the D907 and turn left. At the top of the climb (**2h45min**), you approach two stone pillars on the right and a track signposted 'La Borie de Roque' and 'Camping Vert'. Ignore that track, but take the overgrown grassy track to the right of it. Within 10 minutes you clear the chestnuts and find yourself on top of a ridge, on the old road between La Salvetat and St-Pons. As you head southeast, you pass several old *capitelles* (stone huts similar to bories). The hamlet of Lizarne is seen to the left across the valley, and the farm of La Fourbedié lies below, set like a gem in the midst of tree-darkened slopes. Below it you may notice the scattered remains of the priory of St-Aulary.

At **3h25min** meet a T-junction and turn left downhill. Ignore a grassy track off to the right immediately; keep on the main track (*green* dot waymarks), which doubles back in a U-turn. At a fork about 25 minutes downhill, take the faint grassy track slightly right, uphill. It curves completely round to the right, and in five minutes you come upon a crossing trail at a junction. Now follow the *blue* waymarking round to the left. In under five minutes, having passed a tiny building on the right, *ignore* the path off to the left (even though it is way-marked in blue). Continue downhill in the setting shown here. At a crossroads, turn left downhill and then make your way to the cathedral (**4h 20min**).

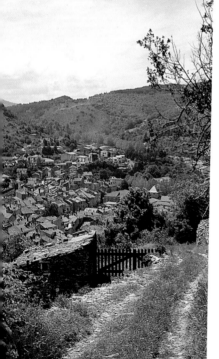

A stony track edged with wild flowers takes you steeply down into St-Pons.

Walk 17: MAZAMET • GORGES DE L'ARNETTE • HAUTPOUL • MAZAMET

Distance: 15km/9.3mi; 4h40min

Grade: moderate-strenuous, with two main ascents (a total of 600m/ 1970ft). The short descent into Mazamet is steep.

Equipment: stout lace-up shoes (walking boots preferable; the path at the start of the walk is very rutted and mucky), sunhat, picnic, water

How to get there: 🚌 to Mazamet. Park in the large car park off Champ de la Ville, northeast of St-Sauveur (No 5 on the Michelin town plan; Car tours 9, 10). Or 🚐 or 🚌 to Mazamet.

Short walk: Gorges de l'Arnette — Hautpoul — Mazamet (9km/ 5.6mi; 2h35min; easy-moderate, with a climb of 280m/920ft at the start; access/equipment as above). From Mazamet take a taxi (arrange at the tourist office, almost opposite St-Sauveur) or ask friends to take you to the junction of the D54 and the road to PIC DE NORE (Car tour 10). Start the walk at the 2h05min-point and walk back to Mazamet.

The ancient fortified village of Hautpoul, a Cathar stronghold (see box page 63) destroyed in 1212, and the bounding Arnette River are the highlights of this circuit — a fascinating introduction to the ecclesiastical and industrial history of the Montagne Noire.

Start out by climbing the Rue du Bassin on the south side of the car park. Turn right at a T-junction and then left. When this tarmac lane ends, climb straight ahead through woods on a footpath damaged by mountain bikes. At **25min** keep ahead on an earthen track. Ten minutes later again keep ahead, where a track goes right to Croix de Prat. Now ignore any paths or tracks off this main track, which is sparingly waymarked in red and white (GR36). At **55min** the walk levels out and you come to a Y-fork. Go right, with a field on your right (there is a red 'X' on the track to left). Passing under oaks you come to the farm of Brettes (**1h10min**).

Walk to the left of the buildings. On the corner of the last building, you will spot a GR waymark: you've joined the GR7 here; turn down the earthen track. Then sneak under an electrified wire and go right on a clear footpath, keeping to right of the field. The gorgeous Arnette Valley opens up below you, all too briefly. Coming into a forest, zigzag downhill through holly and conifers on a beautiful old trail. Nearing the road, you descend beneath false acacias; in summer their white florets are reminiscent of Chinese lanterns.

You drop down to the D54 by one of the old mills (**1h45min**). In the 18th century the nascent textile industry was cradled here, and the wool was washed in the Arnette. With the coming of the machine age, the industry grew so rapidly that a new town had to be built

121

Hautpoul, founded by Visigoths in the 5th century, was later a Saracen lookout guarding this ancient 'salt route' which we descend.

— Mazamet. But the waters of the Arnette were still critical to its success: they now supplied the necessary electricity. Turn left to follow the road beside the river, passing opposite Moulin Maurel, a flower-filled hamlet, and then a grassy riverside verge. Soon the D54 climbs above the river, and you pass the road to Pic de Nore (**2h05min**). *The Short walk begins here.*

Just past this junction you approach a stone wall on the right, marked with a blue arrow. Leave the road just *before* this wall, taking the clear footpath on your right, descending straight into the gorge. *Take care* on this path (you only follow it for a minute, but it is very narrow, and the drop to the right is precipitous). The path takes you to a bridge over the Arnette. Cross the river and then climb a narrow tarmac lane. When you come to a fork, ignore the grassy trail ahead; go left, to climb above a large mill down on the road.

Now the second climb of the walk begins, but this is on a much better footpath. Pass a stream to the right, go through a makeshift gate, then climb through chestnuts, oak, and beech. On reaching a farm (Les Cousteilles; **2h45min**), curl up right between the buildings and leave the farm on a grassy two-wheel track (passing a large garage/barn on right). Ignore the grassy track off to the right just past the farm; keep straight ahead uphill on the motorable track. Then ignore another grassy track into a field; keep climbing under aromatic pines.

At **2h55min** come to the drab chapel of St-Pierre-d'Esplos on the left, with its large cemetery. Curve to the right on a tarmac road, leaving the chapel off to your left. After 200m/yds, by a concrete cross, fork right up a slight incline. (Signs here point to HAUTPOUL and MAZAMET.) Come to another fork, where there is an iron cross: go right. Your route is now a signposted *sentier botanique* (and is *not* correctly drawn on the IGN map). Start the descent, with fields sweeping away to the left. When you come to a three-way fork (about five minutes downhill), ignore the track off left into fields *and* the motorable track straight ahead; take the middle track, which goes half left downhill. In a minute or so *again* take the middle fork. This is still the *sentier botanique*, but it's as stony as a river-bed. Soon come to a well-placed bench looking out across a valley leading into the Arnette. Beyond the bench, at a T-junction, head left downhill. When you come to a crossing track, go straight over and downhill on a footpath. Two minutes later (by a shed on the right with a *chasse privée* sign), continue straight ahead on a track, to a junction with a tarmac road, where you turn right downhill.

Hautpoul

A statue of the Virgin rises on the site of Hautpoul's castle (**3h35min**), destroyed by Simon de Montfort after a seige lasting four days. Turn down right in front of the statue and descend into the village on a narrow lane, passing a tap on your left (at the wc). Wander through the archways and past the old façades and beautiful doorways. A balcony viewpoint overlooks the houses snuggled below the Virgin's rock and the Arnette Valley — from where you can hear the delightful sound of rushing water. And be sure not to miss the overgrown ruins of the Romanesque church of St-Pierre: they are straight ahead as you descend past a shop on the left selling wooden toys and drinks.

Go left through an arch at the end of the village, then turn left down steps leading into a footpath. You descend to the Arnette again. Head off half-right almost at once; you will pass a tiny cemetery on the right as you descend this ancient stone-laid path, the old salt route between Narbonne and the Montagne Noire. Come down to a road just above a weir, passing more attractive mills in ruins. Head left in front of one of them (GR waymark), to cross the river and meet the D54 (**4h**). Now climb the tarmac lane opposite (more GR waymarks). Just after passing a few houses, fork left on a signposted footpath to the ruins of St-Sauveur (**4h15min**), the Cathar church which fell along with the rest of Hautpoul in 1212. It looks out south to the Virgin on the far side of the Arnette and north to Mazamet.

On the return from St-Sauveur, as you approach the road, fork left down a forestry path (GR flash on a light pole ahead). You pick up the old salt route again (photograph page 122), but *take care!* This stone-laid trail is *diabolically* slippery. When you come out to a U-bend in a lane, go left downhill to the river and keep it beside you on the left (go right at a Y-fork by a crucifix). Walk through Place George Tournier and head right at the *mairie*. Make straight for the pointed steeple of Notre-Dame. At a signpost where the Rue des Cordes indicates no entry for motor vehicles, turn right: the car park is just ahead (**4h40min**).

Walk 18: CANAL DU MIDI FROM CARCASSONNE TO TREBES

See also photograph pages 58-59
Distance: 14km/8.7mi; 4h10min   **Grade:** very easy
Equipment: stout lace-up shoes, sunhat, picnic, water
How to get there: 🚌 to La Cité (Porte Narbonnaise; Car tours 9-11).
Or 🚐 or 🚍 to Carcassonne and start at the bridge over the Aude.
To return: 🚐, 🚍 or 🚌 taxi from Trèbes to Carcassonne
Short walk: Trèbes — Ecluse de Villedubert — Trèbes (8km/5mi; 2h; grade/equipment as above). 🚌 to Trèbes (Car tour 10); park near the canal. Follow the canal northwest and then retrace your steps.

The Canal du Midi, one of the most evocative images of the South of France, was created by the ingenuity of one man and the labour of 12,000. Among the obstacles to be overcome was a 174m/570ft-high ridge west of Carcassonne. Paul Riquel, a wealthy tax collector, had the solution: bring in water for the locks from the rushing streams of the Montagne Noire. He even put up a third of the money himself, sacrificing his daughters' dowries. Sadly, he died in 1680 — six months before the canal was opened. With the building of the adjacent Canal Latéral à la Garonne in the 19th century, the link to the Atlantic was complete, fulfilling a dream dating back to Roman times.

Start out at the Porte Narbonnaise, the main gate to La Cité. With your back to the gate, walk left downhill on the road (GR36), keeping the large car park on your right. In two minutes fork left up a path (GR waymark on a lamp-post), to skirt the walls of the citadel. Two minutes later come to a tarmac lane and go left uphill into a square. Walk to the front of the church (St-Gimer),

These arching planes that grace the Canal du Midi near Trèbes were planted to shade the horses that once pulled the barges.

cross the road to the *boulangerie*, and turn right. Go straight over a crossroads; you approach a bridge and a park. Cross another road and go through the park. Turn right under the bridge in the park (Pont Vieux) and then head left down to the track beside the Aude. Turn right on the track and walk under the main N113 road bridge (Pont Neuf). Continue to the next bridge and turn left to cross it (**30min**). On the far side, swing right, back down to the river. Walk under the railway bridge, beyond which the path swings up left. Cross a lane and go straight up a road (GR waymark on a lamp-post on the right). You climb through a housing estate (La Prade); at the first opportunity, turn up right to the main road (D118; you will hear the traffic). Cross the road, drop down to the towpath (**45min**), and turn right. For the next four hours you will amble beside this delightful

waterway, cheering on the rented holiday barges as they navigate the short elliptical locks.

At **1h05min**, at the Ecluse St-Jean, you part company with the GR (the IGN map is out of date). Continuing to the echo of bird-song, you reach a bridge at La Mijane in **1h50min**; this is the halfway point along the canal. At the Ecluse de Villedubert (**3h10min**), Villedubert can be seen across the lock, shaded by palm trees and cypresses. Here you have to leave the canal, but keep along a track going in the same direction; the Aude, and a weir, are just on your right. Continue ahead, at the left-hand side of a quarry, on a track running above the canal. In five minutes you pass the houses of St-Augustin and five minutes later you rejoin the canal.

On coming into Trèbes you approach a bridge; notice the picnic tables on the other side of the canal here. Don't cross the bridge; turn right in front of it, following CARCASSONNE. Soon you will pass a bar on your right (**4h10min**), where you can have a drink and telephone for a taxi. Or, to get to the railway station and bus stops, cross the Aude and continue along the D610 for another 0.5km/10 minutes. (A circular walk, returning along the Aude, would have been ideal, but is not possible; there is nowhere to cross the river between Trèbes and Carcassonne.)

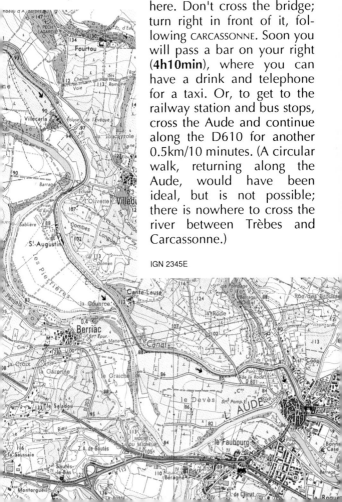

IGN 2345E

Walk 19: CIRCUIT BELOW PEYREPERTUSE

Distance: 4.5km/2.8mi; 2h

Grade: easy, with two short ascents (150m/500ft overall). Some of the paths are narrow; some are stony. There is little shade en route. *Note:* Ignore 'private' signs along this route. Someone has tried to close off the start of the walk with rubbish and warnings about beehives; a few of the early waymarks have been hidden too. But this walk is *very* well waymarked (yellow flashes); if you do not see a waymark in five minutes, you will know you have gone wrong.

Equipment: stout lace-up shoes (walking boots preferable), sunhat, picnic, water

How to get there: 🚌 to Duilhac-sous-Peyrepertuse (Car tour 11). Park on the D14 near the *auberge.*

This walk below Peyrepertuse looks up to the château from the south — not the best vantage point. But the best part of the walk is the 'marble' riverbed of the Verdouble, where it flows in a gorge below the path.

Start out on the D14 at the *auberge;* walk southeast (towards Quéribus) for about 100m/yds, then turn left down a dirt track. (If you come to the *boulangerie,* you have gone too far.) You'll soon see yellow flashes. You follow a track and then leave it, to walk to the right of a vineyard on a footpath. Go through any fence you may encounter, even if it says 'Privé'. (You are likely to find newly-painted waymarks hidden under any 'private'

Waterfalls tumble down the marble-like basin of the emerald Verdouble, sluicing these natural 'Roman baths'. If you do this walk in summer, it should be possible to get to the cascades even though the bridge has collapsed. Walk to the right of the ruined bridge, to a ford. After crossing the river, you can walk past the mill and up the riverbed to the cascades.

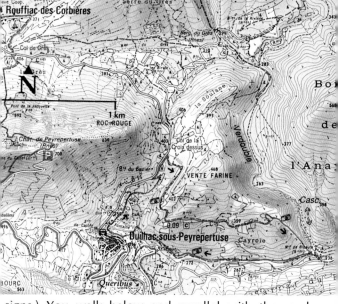

signs.) You walk below and parallel with the road; Peyrepertuse rises above you to the left.

The path curves up to join the road by making a U-turn to the left. Turn right and follow the road 200m/yds to the Col de la Croix Dessus (**35min**). Go right here on a track, following the electricity wires. Now there are good views back to Duilhac, with Peyrepertuse above it. At a U-bend in the track, leave it and follow the footpath ahead for about 15 minutes, enjoying some glimpses of the vineyards in the Verdouble through foliage. When the path at first *seems* to descend, it really climbs up to the left in a tight U-bend, and then descends into the valley. Take care; it's quite stony.

Now the huge gorge of the Verdouble opens up on the left. From the vertiginous edge of the path, you will have the tremendous view shown opposite. On reaching a T-junction with a stony track (**1h05min**), *go left* (ignoring the yellow 'X' on the track). You come to the river, by a caved-in bridge and a sign warning that swimming is forbidden. Across the river is a ruined mill (Moulin de Ribaute). This is a lovely spot for a picnic.

From the bridge return to the T-junction and now go straight ahead. The track soon narrows to a path. Walk to the right of a first vineyard and then go left, to keep a second vineyard on your right. This shady path is a flutter of butterflies. Watch your footing, however; it is narrow in places, with a hefty drop. Having climbed to the D14, turn right. Pass the *boulangerie* and continue to the *auberge* (**2h**).

Glossary

Bartizan: overhanging, battlemented corner turret (of a castle)

Baume: cave, shelter beneath rock

Belvédère: elevated viewpoint

Bergerie: shelter for animals (and sometimes shepherds)

Borie: small dry-stone building, usually with a domed roof (photograph page 23)

Buvette: snack bar

Camelle: pile of salt near salt pans

Capitelle: as borie

Castellas: old ruined castle

Cathars: See box, top of page 63.

Causse: vast limestone plateau; an arid landscape, where most rainfall quickly seeps through the porous rock

Chasse privée: private hunting ground

Cirque: a valley ending in a deep rounded 'amphitheatre' of rock (photograph pages 50-51)

Cité: old term used for a grouping of citizens (as Lavène, Walk 10); also the oldest part of a city (as La Cité at Carcassonne; photograph page 58)

Clos: enclosed parcel of cultivated land (photograph page 41)

Col: depression in a ridge, forming a passage

Dégustation: wine-tasting

Dolmen: prehistoric sepulchral chamber of standing stones supporting a flattish stone 'roof'

Dolomitic rock: rock composed of soluble calcium and less soluble magnesium. The calcium erodes more quickly under the action of rainwater and streams, giving rise to weird formations, for which the French have a very apt name (*ruiniform, qv*).

Domaine: property (vineyard)

Garrigues: limestone wasteland with small pockets of hardy vegetation that can survive the arid conditions. Typical plants include holm oak, box, thistles, gorse, rough grass and wild aromatic plants like lavender, thyme and rosemary. Although these plants are also common to the *maquis*, the *garrigues* are much more open.

Garrigues, Les: an area north of Nîmes, described in Car tour 7, which exhibits the features of the *garrigues*

Gouffre: gulf, abyss

GR (Grande Randonnée): long-distance footpath, waymarked with red and white paint flashes; see page 73.

Grotte: cave

Lavogne: artificial, stone-paved basin for watering livestock

Manade: raising of bulls or horses in the Camargue

Maquis: a dense covering of evergreen plants able to withstand very dry conditions, usually with small hairy or leathery leaves. Includes trees like holm and kermes oaks, junipers, box, strawberry trees, and myrtle, as well as smaller bushes like rosemary, jerusalem sage, broom, heather, and *Cistus*.

Maquis, The: French Resistance during World War II

Mas: country house, usually applied to a farm

Massif: mountain mass with various peaks

Menhir: ancient megalithic standing stone (photograph page 52)

Oppidum: defensive position of dry-stone walls at vantage points. The Ligurians built the first *oppida.*

PR (Petite Randonnée): local waymarked walk, fairly short, often circular; see page 73.

Resurgence: the reappearance above ground of a subterranean water-course; for example, the Fontaine-de-Vaucluse (Car tour 4)

Rive droite, rive gauche: right bank, left bank of a river. (The banks of a river are defined *from* the source.)

Rocher: rock

Ruffes: eroded limestone slopes with a high red clay content, seen in the area of Salagou (photograph page 107).

Ruiniform: a word the French use to describe a chaos of dolomitic rock *(qv),* which has eroded into the shape of ruins. They may look like a building or even a whole town, or sometimes a ruined sculpture. The Cirque de Mourèze (Walk 13, photograph page 11) is a textbook example.

Sentier (botanique): footpath. (A *sentier botanique* usually is accompanied by information panels describing the botany and geology of a specific area; see, for example, Walk 4.)

Table d'orientation: panoramic viewpoint, usually with a circular stone 'table' marked with the points of the compass and pin-pointing the location of towns, mountains, etc.

Via: road. By 100BC Rome held much of the land between the Alps and the Pyrenees. Their most important highways were the *Via Agrippa* via Orange and Avignon to Arles, the *Via Aurelia* via Nice, Fréjus, Aix and Nîmes to Arles and then Spain (today the N7 follows much the same route), and the *Via Domitia* via Sisteron, Apt and Pont Julien south to the *Via Aurelia.*

The slender tower of St-Symphorien rises above oaks near Buoux (Car tour 2 and Walk 3)

✿ Index

Geographical names comprises the only entries in this Index; for non-geographical names, see Contents, page 3. A page number in *italic type* indicates a map; a page number in **bold type** a photograph. Both of these may be in addition to a text reference on the same page.

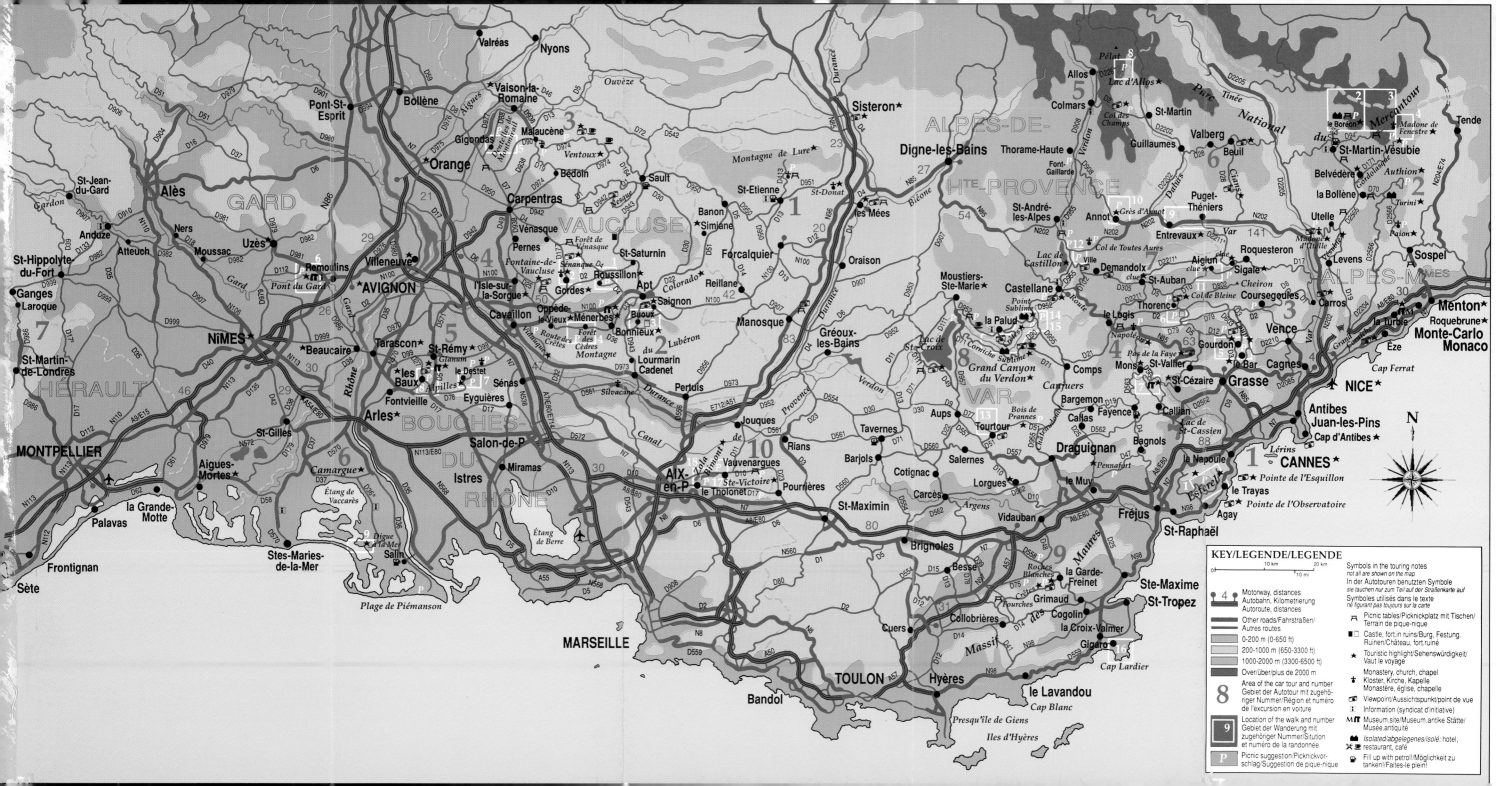

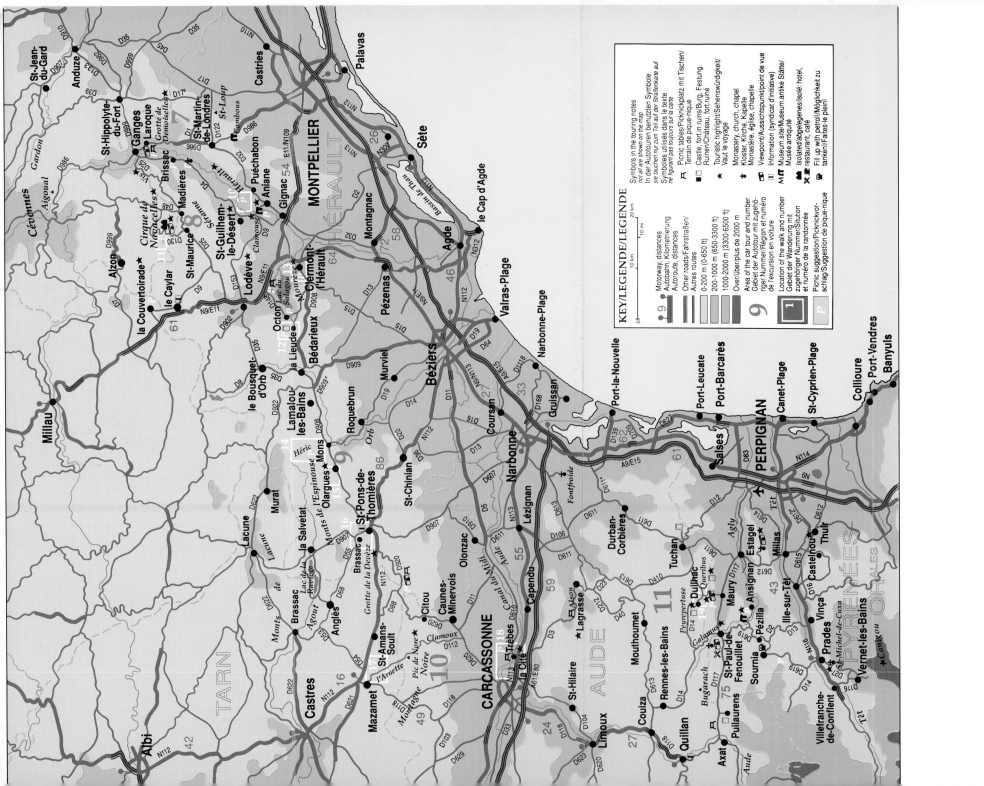